SOMETHING TO HIDE

SOMETHING TO HIDE

A Thriller by

Leslie Sands

JOSEF WEINBERGER PLAYS

LONDON

SOMETHING TO HIDE
First published in 1959
by Josef Weinberger Ltd
(pka English Theatre Guild Ltd)
12-14 Mortimer Street, London, W1T 3JJ
This edition published in 2002

ISBN 0 85676 046 3

SOMETHING TO HIDE was first produced at the Theatre Royal, Windsor, on 3rd February 1958, with the following cast:

HOWARD HOLT	Moray Watson
JULIE	Denise Hirst
KAREN HOLT	Mary Kerridge
INSPECTOR DAVIES	Eynon Evans
MR PURDIE	Leslie Handford
STELLA	Jacqueline Guise
MISS CUNNINGHAM	Elizabeth McKewen

Directed by Joan Riley

SOMETHING TO HIDE subsequently opened at the St. Martin's Theatre, London, on Tuesday evening, 29th April 1958, with the following cast:

HOWARD HOLT	Michael Gough
JULIE	Audrey Nicholson
KAREN HOLT	Mary Kerridge
INSPECTOR DAVIES	Alan Webb
MR PURDIE	Frank Pettitt
STELLA	Jacqueline Guise
MISS CUNNINGHAM	Elizabeth McKewen

Produced and directed by Joan Riley
Designed by Carl Toms

SYNOPSIS OF SCENES

The action takes place in the living room of a converted toll-house in Essex. The time is the present.

ACT ONE

A night in September.

ACT TWO

Scene One	A few days later.
Scene Two	Some weeks later.

ACT THREE

Scene One	Shortly afterwards.
Scene Two	The next morning.

ACT ONE

The Toll House at Kingsmead in Essex is a charming old property which has been transformed with care and taste into a luxurious weekend retreat. The large living room is its main feature. It has a front door URC which opens on from a small but attractive garden; tall, built-in bookshelves in the back wall; two carpeted steps ascending to a door UL that opens off to the main bedroom; a handsome bay window DR looking out on the Essex countryside; and across the room a lesser door L, which opens off to the kitchen and other offices. The fireplace is understood to be DC. Behind one of the pictures is a concealed modern safe, built into the thick wall.

The furnishings are costly and well-chosen. A comfortable settee is LC and has a bright, loose cover to match the curtains; below it a low table holds matches, ashtray and assorted magazines. A big easy chair stands RC with a small occasional table on its R. A small armchair DL faces in. At R, set slightly in from the window and in line with the right wall, is an expensive desk or writing table of wood, with its chair set in-stage so that anyone sitting at the desk is seen in profile and directly faces the window. On the desk are two large and individually framed photographs (head and shoulders) of HOWARD *and* KAREN HOLT, *a large tooled-leather blotter with sideleaves, writing implements and a modern telephone. Elsewhere, a radio, a table or chest with drinks, a wastepaper basket, telephone directories, notebooks, scripts and varied files.* HOWARD'S *portable typewriter, fitted with a sheet of paper, is on the chair DL.*

As the lights rise the radio plays soft dance music as HOWARD *and* JULIE *stand kissing in close embrace C.* HOWARD HOLT *is a good-looking man in the early thirties, with more than his fair share of virile charm.* JULIE GRANT *is an attractive and vivacious redhead, younger than* HOLT *by a good ten years. She has had a drink or two but does not show any obvious effects. Her coat is round her shoulders. Their kiss ends.*

HOWARD   . . . and nobody would be any wiser.

JULIE   (*edgy*) How about that drink?

HOWARD   Sorry. (*To drinks.*) You put it clean out of my mind.

JULIE   Thanks for the compliment – (*Turns.*) – or is it?

HOWARD   ~~Whisky?~~ *Red wine*

JULIE   It used to be champagne.

HOWARD   Still can be, if you want it.

JULIE   ~~Whisky~~'s fine. *Red wine's*

          (*He pours, as she lights a cigarette she has taken from her case.*)

JULIE   I'll have to watch my drinking from now on, as well as my smoking.

          (*She shrugs out of her coat. He makes no reply, busy with the drinks. She switches off the radio.*)

JULIE   Never thought it could happen, did we?

HOWARD   It was on the cards, always; what people call "the natural course of events".

JULIE   When you're married, yes: when you're not, they call it damned carelessness. Sorry I threw it in your face like that, the moment I arrived – I just couldn't keep it to myself any longer.

HOWARD   Who else have you told?

JULIE   Nobody. I've been as quiet as the grave. Except the doctor. ~~Don't frown, he didn't know me from Adam. I found him in the phone book and paid him on the spot.~~ *I even got the test from a different chemist*

HOWARD   ~~But you had to give your name?~~

JULIE   ~~Not the real one: that came out of the book, too.~~

HOWARD	(*hands drink*) Clever girl.
JULIE	Not clever – discreet. A word I learned from you.
HOWARD	Cheers.
JULIE	~~Mud in your eye.~~ *Cheers*
	(*She drinks; he doesn't.*)
HOWARD	Your landlady?
JULIE	She knows. Oh, she hasn't put it into words, but she knows. You can't fool the Mrs Ramsays of this world. After all, she's had three herself, two ~~on the wrong side of the blanket.~~ *from different fathers*
HOWARD	Don't talk like that –
JULIE	You think I'm any better?
HOWARD	Julie, I've told you everything can be taken care of –
JULIE	Not that way, ~~not the way you said.~~ *I won't let it*
HOWARD	*because* ~~It won't be like that, I promise.~~
JULIE	I won't let it – because I'm going through with this, really right through. I haven't done much that's decent with my life. Perhaps this'll make up for it, somehow.
HOWARD	I know how you feel.
JULIE	Do you? If only you did, and if only you felt the same.
HOWARD	What then?

JULIE   Why say it. You've heard it all before, too many times. (*A plea.*) Darling, I wouldn't care how we lived –

HOWARD   That's out of the question.

JULIE   For you, yes; but what about me?

HOWARD   I can't reorganise my whole life.

JULIE   I'll *have* to reorganise mine. (*No answer.*) I know it's no good – you couldn't give it up, could you? All this . . . the house in London . . . winters abroad . . . fine friends and ritzy living. You'd never give it up, not for a tramp like me. (*Stubs cigarette out.*)

HOWARD   It isn't mine to give. Everything belongs to Karen – everything. And the money that goes with it – money we both need.

JULIE   People get along without money.

HOWARD   Not my sort of people, or yours. It's a long time since you tried, I've seen to that.

JULIE   You've still got your books –

HOWARD   Not without Karen.

JULIE   She doesn't write them.

HOWARD   She publishes, that's the part that counts.

JULIE   There must be other publishers.

HOWARD   I tried them all before I met her. You don't understand, Julie – without Karen, I'm nothing. Why do you think I married her in the first place?

JULIE   That's something you've never admitted before – not in so many words.

HOWARD   Leave me a little pride. I haven't much – just
            enough to make me rather ashamed of being a
            kept man.

JULIE   But not ashamed enough to do anything about
            it.

            (*She breaks away to the desk.*)

JULIE   She'd never let you go, anyway.

HOWARD   No?

JULIE   No, Howard. Shall I tell you why? She's years
            older than you are, and a lot less –
            complicated. In a set-up like that if she's lucky
            enough to wear a wedding ring a woman hangs
            on good and hard; especially if she's married
            to a nice, good-looking swine like you.

HOWARD   Thank you. (*Lightly.*) Another drink?

JULIE   (*at portrait*) There she sits, the mighty Karen
            Holt, mistress of all she surveys. She's got
            everything – money, success and you. And
            she's going to hang on to every little bit of it –
            for good.

HOWARD   (*takes her glass*) How many did you have on
            the way?

JULIE   A girl in my condition needs a little
            consolation.

            (*He picks up the photograph and slips it
            carelessly into a desk drawer, closing it
            casually.*)

HOWARD   Better?

JULIE   *Much better.* (*Puts arms round him.*) Now
            there's only the two of us, together. (*Nestles.*)
            That's the way I like it.

(He kisses her forehead.)

JULIE   Sorry I lashed out like that.

HOWARD Let's forget it for tonight. We've got the whole weekend to talk things over, make our plans.

JULIE   It won't be much like all the others –

HOWARD It needn't be less enjoyable.

(He kisses her properly, and this time she responds.)

HOWARD I'll get you that drink.

JULIE   I'd rather have a cigarette.

(He checks in the cigarette box on the desk.)

HOWARD Sorry – ~~run out.~~

JULIE   ~~Me too~~!

HOWARD ~~I'll try the bedroom~~ –

JULIE   Don't worry. I've got a box of fifty in the car. I bought them on the way. *(Puts coat around shoulders.)* ~~I never could smoke those things of yours anyway~~.

HOWARD Be careful.

JULIE   Nobody's going to spot me – I'll slip out like a thief in the night.

HOWARD *(to her)* Better let me –

JULIE   Stop worrying! Discretion's my middle name, and you know what they say – discretion is the better part of –

HOWARD *(puts finger to her lips)* Not being found out.

(She snaps her teeth at it, smiles and runs out. His own smile fades as the door closes and he looks thoughtful as he splashes soda in his drink and switches on the music again. It fades in immediately, soft and romantic. Suddenly, front outside comes the sharp screech of powerful brakes. A second later, a car door slams. HOWARD goes to the window and lifts a curtain to peer out. Outside all is dark. The front door opens and he turns, dropping the curtain. KAREN HOLT, his wife, rushes in. She is a well-groomed woman of forty who has just received a severe shock and is in a state bordering on nervous collapse.)

HOWARD   Karen!

KAREN   Oh, Howard! Howard, darling –

HOWARD   What on earth are you doing here?

KAREN   You've got to help me –

HOWARD   What is it?

KAREN   There's been an accident. We must get on to the police.

            (She lunges towards the phone.)

HOWARD   Wait.

KAREN   No. There's no time. Operator – operator –

            (She feverishly works the receiver hook. He crosses quickly and takes the phone from her.)

HOWARD   You're not going to talk to anyone in that state.

            (He closes the door behind her.)

KAREN   I must!

(He replaces it and guides her to a chair.)

HOWARD   Sit down, I'll get you a drink.

KAREN   But the police –

HOWARD   Karen, *please*.

            (He sits and gives her brandy.)

HOWARD   No – tell me exactly what happened.

KAREN   She came from nowhere.

HOWARD   She – who? (*Rises.*) Who are you talking
            about?

KAREN   The girl outside: I ran her down.

            *(He makes a move for the door. She rises
            quickly.)*

KAREN   It was an accident– it wasn't my fault – you
            must believe me.

HOWARD   (*turns*) Darling, of course I believe you, but –

KAREN   She ran right in front of the car, I – it wasn't my
            fault.

            (She almost faints and he catches her.)

HOWARD   Hey, you'd better lie down. I'll take care of
            this.

            (He helps her towards the bedroom.)

KAREN   We must get help –

HOWARD   I'll see to it: you go in the bedroom and lie
            down.

KAREN   But she's lying out there in the road –

HOWARD	Do as I say, and don't come out.
KAREN	What if she's – badly hurt?
HOWARD	Leave everything to me.

(She goes off and he shuts the door behind her, then crosses to pick up JULIE'S *handbag which* KAREN *has failed to notice. On his way to the door he remembers the girl's glass and returns to run his handkerchief quickly round the rim before replacing it on the drinks tray. With a final hurried glance round, he goes out of the front door. The romantic melody ends. A slight 'ping' comes from the phone. Immediately, a fresh tune bursts from the radio. In contrast, it is loud and rhythmic. A few moments later.* KAREN *re-enters. She is still badly shaken, and walks unsteadily to the settee to sit in a fever of anxiety, her fingers pressed to her brow. The blaring jazz beats into her brain and she crosses to switch it off.* HOWARD *returns.)*

HOWARD	I told you not to come out.
KAREN	*(whispers) How is she?*
HOWARD	*(quietly)* I think her neck's broken – she's dead.

*(*KAREN *gives a low moan of horror and moves quickly towards the door. He restrains her.)*

HOWARD	Don't go out there.
KAREN	I must!
HOWARD	There's nothing you can do: everything will be taken care of.
KAREN	But Howard –
HOWARD	*(seats her)* Sit down and tell me – where did

she come from?

KAREN   Out of the dark, that's all I know – dead!

HOWARD   Steady. Think, carefully. Was she alone?

KAREN   Yes.

HOWARD   You didn't see anyone else?

KAREN   No.

HOWARD   There's nobody out there now. Were you seen driving up?

KAREN   It's pitch-black, I haven't passed a car for miles. But darling, the police –

HOWARD   We're not going to tell the police. There'll be no witnesses, no trace. I've moved her.

KAREN   (*dazed*) Howard, we can't!

HOWARD   Why not?

KAREN   We must tell them –

HOWARD   You killed her.

KAREN   By accident.

HOWARD   Accident or not, *you killed her*.

KAREN   It wasn't my fault –

HOWARD   Try proving that without a witness! What if they prosecute?

KAREN   Prosecute? Why should they?

HOWARD   You haven't the ghost of an excuse, you've driven in here a thousand times. You came a steep hill and took a corner too fast: a girl was

on the road, you knocked her down. She's
dead. They'll call it manslaughter.

KAREN   No!

HOWARD   They'll call it manslaughter and you'll go to
prison – *if they find out*.

KAREN   They already know!

(*His face changes.*)

HOWARD   You telephoned?

KAREN   While you were out, from the phone in the
bedroom.

HOWARD   I asked you to leave everything to me!

KAREN   Darling, they're bound to find out sooner or
later. You can't cover up a thing like this and
pretend it never happened –

HOWARD   We've got to. Don't you understand? I've
moved her. That alters everything. I did it for
you, for your sake – but what d'you suppose
they'll make of it?

KAREN   (*eyes closed*) I – can't think –

HOWARD   Quickly! How much did you tell them?

KAREN   I believe I said –

HOWARD   The exact words.

KAREN   I said, "Can you come at once? There's been an
accident."

HOWARD   You didn't say she was dead?

KAREN   I didn't know.

HOWARD   Did you mention the girl at all?

KAREN   No. I was too upset.

HOWARD   They must have asked for details.

KAREN   Yes, but I broke down. Sergeant Briggs said
         he'd come at once.

HOWARD   And there was nothing about the girl – not one
         word – you're absolutely sure?

KAREN   (*nods*) I – couldn't speak.

HOWARD   So he doesn't know what kind of accident: that
         helps. (*Paces.*) Suppose you hit the gate as
         you came in, an error of judgement –

KAREN   I've driven in a thousand times, you said so.

HOWARD   But if the car went suddenly out of control –

KAREN   There's nothing wrong with the car, Howard –

HOWARD   Suppose the light was bad, you couldn't see
         properly?

KAREN   There's plenty of light. It's a dangerous bend,
         that's why they put the street lamp there.

HOWARD   The lamp outside! If that failed for some reason
         anyone could smash into it. That would leave
         the car lying half out in the road.

KAREN   The lamp was on – it's on still.

         (*He moves for his raincoat, which is lying over
         the back of a chair.*)

HOWARD   That can be taken care of.

KAREN   (*rises*) Darling, this is madness.

HOWARD   It's a chance worth taking.

KAREN   But the police are on their way.

HOWARD   You'll have to handle that side of it. I've got to fix the car and get the girl away.

KAREN   What if they find out later?

HOWARD   (*struggles into coat*) They won't. We're not up against Scotland Yard, just one old country policeman.

KAREN   Howard, I can't!

HOWARD   (*to her*) Now listen carefully. You drove up here alone, the lamp was out and you smashed into it. You ran in to tell me but I wasn't here. Remember that, it's important – ~~I'll find the answer later~~. You telephoned them at once because the car's a dangerous obstruction. To back that up, ring the garage as soon as I've gone and get Will Purdie to come over.

KAREN   He'll be shut now.

HOWARD   (*thrusts directory at her*) Get him at his home, ~~he can't live far away~~!

                  (*Shocked at the sudden harshness of his tone she stares at him, her head whirling. The directory falls to her feet. Softening, he holds her shoulders.*)

HOWARD   Steady, Karen. You've got to keep your nerve, everything depends on that.

KAREN   But I don't understand –

HOWARD   It's better this way – believe me.

KAREN   (*breathes*) All right – I'll try.

HOWARD   Good girl.

(*He picks up the phone book and gives it to her.*)

HOWARD   Now give me the keys – the car keys.

KAREN   I left them out there.

(*He goes to the door.*)

HOWARD   I'll be back as soon as I can. (*Turns.*) If things turn awkward, stall him. Tell him you're badly shaken up, you'll go down to the police station tomorrow. (*She nods, dumbly. He looks at her for a split second, then goes, swiftly.*)

KAREN   Howard!

(*The door closes behind him. She realises she is holding the directory and puts it on the desk to look for a number. She closes the book and opens the cigarette box. It is empty. She gets a cigarette from her bag and lifts the phone. Outside, a powerful car starts up, grinds a short way in reverse then changes up and moves forward in low gear. KAREN has covered the mouthpiece with her hand. There is a heavy crash, not too near, followed by the tinkle of breaking glass. KAREN puts the phone to her ear.*)

KAREN   Yes, I'm sorry. I want Kingsmead one-two, please. (*As she waits she lights her cigarette with a table-lighter from the desk.*)

KAREN   Oh, isn't there? He must be there by now, it's – (*Checks watch.*) – nearly ten past ten. Well, would you try double-three? Thank you.

(*Something outside draws her head round. Again she covers the phone as she listens carefully. Then she goes back to it.*)

KAREN   Oh – hello. Is that the garage? Will, this is Mrs Holt. That's right. I've been trying to get you

at your home but – oh, I see. I need help, Will,
badly. There's been a smash and my car's
jammed outside – I think it should be moved at
once. Yes, I've done that, they're coming over.
Would you? I'd be so grateful. Thank you,
Will. Goodbye.

(*She hangs up and crosses to the mirror to
make quick repairs to her make-up. She is
calming, gradually. She glances round the
room, tidies a magazine that has fallen to the
floor, then finds her handbag and takes out a
brown leather folder which holds her driving
licence. As she lays this, open, on the table,
something in the ashtray catches her eye. She
lifts the ashtray as the door buzzer goes. She
replaces it, straightens her dress and crosses
to the door.*)

DAVIES   (*off*) Mrs Holt?

KAREN   Yes.

DAVIES   (*off*) Good evening, madam. My name is Davies.
Inspector Davies.

KAREN   (*surprised*) Oh! Do come in.

DAVIES   (*enters*) Thank you.

(*He comes into the room, screwing up his eyes
slightly at the sudden change of light.* WALTER
DAVIES *is a burly, middle-aged family man,
with a likeable grin and a deceptive
gentleness of manner. His Northern accent
must be real, and not comic.*)

DAVIES   (*looks round appreciatively*) My word, this is a
bit of all right, isn't it? Surprising what can be
done with these old places nowadays.

KAREN   Won't you sit down?

DAVIES   No thanks. I shan't be stopping long.

KAREN   This is rather unexpected – I thought Sergeant
                Briggs was coming.

DAVIES   Tom's outside, checking up on the damage. I
                happened to be in the station when you
                telephoned, and volunteered to run him over in
                the car – that old bike's a bit hard on his
                rheumatics.

KAREN   How kind. I wondered how you got here so
                quickly.

DAVIES   (*twinkles*) One thing about the police force,
                madam – the men might be lacking but the
                transport's wonderful.

KAREN   Can I offer you a drink, Inspector?

DAVIES   Well, you could – but I think we'd better get
                down to business first. (*Notebook out.*) I
                promised Tom I'd take down the particulars to
                save time.

KAREN   Of course.

                (*As he turns the pages of his note book she
                reaches for her cigarettes.*)

KAREN   Cigarette?

DAVIES   No thanks. I smoke a pipe.

KAREN   You're new to this district, aren't you?

DAVIES   (*feels for pencil*) Not entirely. I'm from
                headquarters at Chelmsford. Kingsmead's part
                of my division, though I don't get over very
                often. I'm making inquiries on a job at the
                Grange.

KAREN   I see.

DAVIES	Now then. I've got your number. You were driving the car yourself, I take it?
KAREN	That's correct.
DAVIES	And you telephoned us straightaway?
KAREN	Almost immediately.
DAVIES	That was at two minutes past ten. This little schemozzle must have taken place about ten o'clock, then?
KAREN	I expect so. I didn't notice the time – is it important?
DAVIES	Not as a rule, but we always like to know. Can I see your driving licence?
KAREN	I have it ready. (*Passes it over.*)
DAVIES	Thank you. (*Consults it.*) This seems to be a London address?
KAREN	Yes, my home's in London. I only come here occasionally for weekends.
DAVIES	(*writes*) Ah.
KAREN	Actually, the place belongs to Howard, my husband. He's a writer.
DAVIES	Yes, so they tell me.
KAREN	My father bought the property originally and had it converted ready for his retirement. But no one could ever stop him working and so when he died and I took over the business I passed this place on to Howard as somewhere he could come and work, in peace.
DAVIES	I wish my wife'd give me a country seat. When I want peace and quiet I have to go and sit in the greenhouse.

KAREN   Bad luck.

DAVIES   (*hands licence back*) That's all in order – no
            endorsements, anyway.

KAREN   I've been lucky.

DAVIES   What about your insurance certificate?

KAREN   That's here too, somewhere.

            (*She feels in a pocket of the folder and
            produces it. He scans it.*)

DAVIES   All present and correct. Made many claims
            lately?

KAREN   This will be the first ever.

DAVIES   Then you shouldn't have much trouble. (*Still
            writing.*) No personal injury sustained . . .

KAREN   No, thank goodness.

DAVIES   And nobody else involved . . .

KAREN   Why do you ask?

DAVIES   (*glances up*) Routine.

KAREN   Nobody, I'm happy to say.

DAVIES   You were alone in the car?

KAREN   (*nods*) Quite alone.

DAVIES   (*writes*) No – witnesses.

KAREN   No.

DAVIES   No. There never are.

KAREN   There wasn't a soul about. This is a lonely
               spot, especially at night.

DAVIES   You're telling me. All these tall trees, and night
               owls. Enough to give you the willies.

KAREN   You're not a local, man, Inspector?

DAVIES   No, I come from the North, where you can see a
               decent hill or two. Down here it's as flat as a
               pancake – as my wife says, you can see round
               every corner before you come to it.

KAREN   But the soil's good – as a gardener you must
               admit that.

DAVIES   Too damp for my liking. Nothing but mud and
               swamp all the way to the coast. That's why
               you've never had a decent football team in
               these parts – you can't keep 'em upright long
               enough to train 'em.

KAREN   It can't be as bad as all that.

DAVIES   Just you try driving round these roads in
               winter, chasing poachers.

KAREN   There you have me. We usually winter in town
               on the Continent.

DAVIES   Very nice, too, if you call get used to driving
               on the wrong side of the road.

KAREN   It doesn't worry me.

DAVIES   You must be a good driver.

KAREN   I've had a car for twelve or fifteen years.

DAVIES   How did you manage this little mix-up, then?

KAREN   Oh – took the corner too fast, I suppose.
               Overconfident. You know what women drivers
               are.

DAVIES	I could write a book. (*To phone.*) I'd better arrange to have it shifted, it's not very safe where it is. (*Lifts phone.*)
KAREN	I've done that. The garage man's on his way now.
DAVIES	Oh? You didn't waste much time.
KAREN	I thought it best to have it moved as soon as possible.
DAVIES	A pity everybody isn't as conscientious. Well, I think that's about all. I'll put the usual report in and you'd better contact your insurance company, if you haven't done so already.

(*She darts a glance at him but he is smiling innocently as he puts his notebook away.*)

KAREN	I'll give them a ring first thing in the morning. Now, what about that drink?

(*He scratches his ear with the pencil point.*)

DAVIES	I don't know that I should, really.
KAREN	Not unless you've quite finished, of course?
DAVIES	(*pockets pencil*) I never did believe in flogging to death.
KAREN	That's more like it. What will you have – gin, or sherry?
DAVIES	That's quite a selection. I wouldn't say no to a nice bottle of beer.
KAREN	I expect there's some in the kitchen. Excuse me.
DAVIES	Certainly.

(She goes off, L. He smacks his lips then strolls to the open door.)

DAVIES   Tom!

VOICE   *(off)* Yes, sir?

DAVIES   How long do you think you'll be?

VOICE   Five minutes?

DAVIES   Take your time.

(He begins to close the door and then a sudden thought makes him peep out again. He considers for a moment, then shuts it and takes out his pipe. Sucking at the stem reflectively he moves down and studies HOWARD's picture as KAREN comes back with two small bottles and a pewter tankard on a tray.)

KAREN   Light ale?

DAVIES   Just the job.

(She sets the tray down, opens one of the bottles and pours.)

KAREN   How about Tom Briggs?

DAVIES   Better not. I think he's had his pint.

KAREN   I thought you were doing the driving?

DAVIES   Aye, but he's doing the night duty. This'll be your husband, then?

KAREN   Yes, that's Howard.

DAVIES   Good looking chap.

KAREN   I think so.

DAVIES   He's written quite a few books, they tell me.

KAREN   Yes, he's a novelist.

DAVIES   Thrillers?

KAREN   No – romance, light fiction.

DAVIES   Pity.

KAREN   Why?

DAVIES   I've always wanted to meet one of these detective writers and tell him what I think about their comic policemen.

KAREN   (*smiles, handing him the beer*) There you are.

DAVIES   Thanks very much.

KAREN   Why not sit down and enjoy it?

DAVIES   Might as well. (*Sits.*) Is he about?

KAREN   Howard? No, I'm afraid he's out.

DAVIES   Oh.

KAREN   He wasn't expecting me, you see. I had a board meeting fixed for tomorrow morning but it was cancelled at the last moment. I suddenly took it into my head to drive down for the weekend.

DAVIES   The change'll do you good. All the best.

KAREN   Cheers. (*He drinks, then lowers the tankard, looking into it.*)

KAREN   I hope it's all right?

DAVIES   As good as you'll get – down here.

          (*He drinks again. The door buzzer goes.*)

KAREN	That'll be Mr Purdie.

(She answers it.)

KAREN   Come in, Will.

(WILL PURDIE *enters, a grizzled man in faded overalls and a small, oil-stained beret.*)

WILL   'Evening.

DAVIES 'Evening.

WILL   *(spots him)* Blimey! Didn't take you long, did it?

KAREN   You two must know each other?

WILL   Not 'arf. How's the copper trade?

DAVIES Mustn't grumble. How's the motor swindle?

WILL   Shocking.

KAREN   Can I get you a drink, Will?

WILL   No thanks, mum, haven't got time – the missus is waiting for me back at the garage.

KAREN   Then we mustn't keep you. Have you had a look at the car?

WILL   I'll say! How d'you manage it?

KAREN   Pure carelessness, I'm afraid.

WILL   I couldn't believe me own eyes! *(To DAVIES.)* She's a smashing driver, as a rule. *(Turns back to KAREN with a grin.)* And 'ere – what's the Council going to say about that lamp?

KAREN   I hope they won't be too hard on me: if it hadn't been out in the first place I'd never had gone into it.

DAVIES   (*suddenly*) Out?

KAREN   (*slight pause*) Didn't I mention that?

DAVIES   (*amiably*) No, I don't believe you did. I'd
            better make a note. (*He does so.*)

KAREN   How's the family, Will?

WILL   First-rate! I'm a grandfather now, you know.

KAREN   No, I didn't!

WILL   Middle of August – my little Elsie had twins.

KAREN   Congratulations.

WILL   Mind you, it's a mixed blessing – two mouths
            to feed instead of one. Still, she gets the family
            allowance right away.

KAREN   I must call and see her over the weekend.

WILL   Would you, mum? She's be tickled pink. She's
            a good girl is Elsie, one of the best. I was
            saying to my Gert only the other day –

DAVIES   I don't want to interrupt but I thought you
            were pressed for time?

WILL   Never let you rest, do they? (*To* DAVIES.) I'm
            only waiting for your kind permission to
            remove the debris.

DAVIES   Go on, then, get cracking; but check with Tom
            Briggs first.

WILL   Right. (*To door.*) It won't take long – I've got
            the breakdown van outside.

KAREN   Thank you, Will. I'm sorry to have brought you
            out so late.

WILL   'Salright, mum – I was working over, anyway.
            Gert had just brought my supper down on her
            bike.

KAREN   And I interrupted it!

WILL   No, you didn't! I finished it before I came, and
            brought the afters with me.

            (*He produces a bottle of stout from his pocket,
            winks and nips out. DAVIES rises.*)

DAVIES   Time I was making tracks myself.

KAREN   Won't you have the other one?

DAVIES   No thanks. Better save it for your husband,
            he's going to need that when he hears about
            his car.

KAREN   The car's mine. Howard doesn't drive much.

DAVIES   Ah, of course: your name on the insurance. (*He
            fingers his hat thoughtfully.*)

KAREN   Anything worrying you, Inspector?

DAVIES   No I wouldn't say that – but about that street
            lamp you say it was out when you turned the
            corner?

KAREN   It must have been. I know I didn't see it.

DAVIES   Weren't you using your headlights?

KAREN   Yes, Of course. (*The slightest pause.*) But they
            were dipped.

DAVIES   You'd just come up a fairly steep hill, travelling
            at speed –

KAREN   I had them on then of course, but I always
            lower them when I reach the bend. A sudden
            dazzle on that corner could prove fatal.

DAVIES   True enough.

KAREN   I nearly ran into a car once, coming the
              opposite way. I've dipped my headlights ever
              since to make the turn.

DAVIES   Even so, you came round at quite a lick – you
              must have done, to pile the car up like that.

KAREN   I'm so used to driving in I suppose I took it for
              granted.

DAVIES   That's only natural. You probably sensed
              something was wrong but it was too late to do
              anything about it?

KAREN   That's it exactly.

DAVIES   Even to brake?

KAREN   I did try – but I must have been going too fast.

DAVIES   (*nods*) All I can say is, you're lucky to have
              walked away from a smash like that.

KAREN   I was badly shaken up.

DAVIES   Yes, Tom told me what a state you were in
              when you telephoned. I suppose you left
              everything just as it was outside?

KAREN   I thought it best.

DAVIES   We always appreciate that. (*Near window.*) But
              in that case, why are the headlights on now –
              at full? (*Pause.*) See for yourself.

              (*He yanks the curtain back. The room is
              flooded with powerful light.*)

KAREN   I – went out and adjusted them afterwards.

DAVIES   Afterwards?

KAREN   After I telephoned. I realised the car couldn't
              be left like that, a dangerous obstruction on
              such a narrow bend and thought it advisable to
              as much light as possible until it could be
              moved. I went out and saw to it before I rang
              the garage.

DAVIES   (*grins*) That explains it.

              (*A knock at the door.* WILL *looks in.*)

WILL   'Scuse me, mum – could I have the keys?

KAREN   Didn't I leave them out there?

WILL   No. She's all locked up.

KAREN   (*after a slight hesitation*) They must be in my
              bag – now where did I put it?

DAVIES   Would this be it?

              (*He passes her brown leather handbag.*)

KAREN   Yes, thank you. (*Pretends to search.*) No . . .
              they don't seem to be there. How silly of me, I
              expect I put them down somewhere. I –

              (HOWARD'S *voice is heard, off.*)

HOWARD   (*off*) Karen –

              (*He appears in the doorway.*)

HOWARD   Karen, are you all right?

DAVIES   I'm afraid your wife's had a spot of bother, Mr
              Holt.

HOWARD   Briggs told me. You're the inspector?

DAVIES   Yes, sir. Davies.

HOWARD   (*to* KAREN) Darling, are you sure you're not
              hurt?

KAREN   Yes, Howard, I'll explain later. They're waiting
              to take the car away and somehow, stupidly,
              I've mislaid my keys.

HOWARD   (*blandly*) Use mine.

              (*He feels in his raincoat pocket and takes out
              a set on a smart brown leather tag which he
              hands to* DAVIES.)

DAVIES   Here you are, Will – catch!

              (*He tosses them across.*)

WILL   (*catches them*) Now we're away! I'll give you a
              ring tomorrow, mum, and let you know the
              damage.

DAVIES   And go easy on the estimate – remember the
              Council might have to pay for that lamp.

WILL   You're breaking my heart. Goodnight, all.

HOWARD   Anything else you want, Inspector?

DAVIES   No, I think we've covered everything.

KAREN   I've been going through quite a cross-
              examination, Howard.

DAVIES   (*laughs*) My fault, I'm afraid. I get so used to
              asking questions it's become a habit.

HOWARD   But you're perfectly satisfied now?

DAVIES   I think so.

HOWARD   (*crosses to door*) Thank you very much.
              Inspector, and goodnight. (*Opens it.*)

DAVIES	Good night, madam. (*Crosses to* HOWARD.) Good night, sir. (*Turns.*) By the way, Mr Holt – do you always carry keys to your wife's car?
HOWARD	Usually, why?
DAVIES	She says you don't drive much.
HOWARD	That's true. (*Smiles.*) So what?
DAVIES	Oh – nothing. (*Grins.*) Damn silly question, when you come to think of it! Goodnight.

(*He goes. Pause.*)

HOWARD	Everything all right?
KAREN	(*sits*) I think so. He brought Briggs up in his car.
HOWARD	I know. I saw them coming up the hill and had to hide; that's why I couldn't get the keys back.
KAREN	They arrived so quickly I didn't have time to go outside and check –
HOWARD	Never mind that now – you got away with it.
KAREN	I hope so. Oh, God – I hope so.

(*He goes to the window and peeps through the curtains.*)

HOWARD	They've gone. Everything's quiet. It's all over, where you're concerned.

(KAREN *relaxes as the tension begins to leave her: then she sees him moving to the door, and rises.*)

KAREN	Darling, don't go out again!

HOWARD   I must. I only came back to let you have the
              keys.

KAREN   Please!

HOWARD   (*to her*) I've got some unfinished business,
              remember? Something that won't wait.

              (*She turns away, sickened. He puts his arms
              round her.*)

HOWARD   Steady.

KAREN   What have we done? (*Head back.*) Dear God,
              what have we done?

HOWARD   Listen, Karen. (*Turns her to face him.*) You've
              got to forget tonight, forget it quickly, while
              you can. It's too late to change anything and
              there's no going back.

KAREN   Hold me – hold me close.

              (*He embraces her.*)

KAREN   Tell me that you love me.

HOWARD   Darling –

KAREN   Say it, Howard. Say it – please.

HOWARD   You know I do.

KAREN   (*looks up at him*) That's all that matters.

              (*He presses his cheek to hers then draws back
              gently.*)

HOWARD   I must go. I'll be late. Try and get some rest.

              (*He goes towards the door.*)

KAREN   Darling –

(*He turns. She goes to him.*)

KAREN   Be careful – for my sake.

(*He takes her chin in his hand and kisses her
tenderly – then he goes. Left alone,* KAREN
*stretches wearily, then comes to look at his
portrait. She picks it up and holds it lovingly
for a moment. As she replaces it she notices
her own picture is missing from its accustomed
place. She looks round the room, puzzled, then
her gaze rests on the desk drawer which is not
properly shut. She pulls it open and takes out
her own photograph. About to put it in its
normal position she halts and looks round at
the ashtray she considered earlier, then
returns the portrait to the drawer, closes it,
and crosses to pick the ashtray up. She takes
from it* JULIE'S *cigarette end, which is
cork-tipped. Putting the ashtray down she
faces front, looking at the butt . . . then,
slowly, begins to tear it to shreds.*)

(*Blackout.*)

ACT TWO

Scene One

*The same. A few days later. The Holt's new maid is answering
the telephone.* STELLA *is a local girl, pretty and full of
self-confidence. She has been interrupted in her work and her
dusters and cleaning-cloths are close at hand.* HOWARD'S
typewriter is on the desk.

STELLA   I'm ever so sorry – no, he isn't. Mr Holt's been
                out all morning and I don't know when he'll be
                back. Hard to say, you can't always tell with Mr
                Holt – lunchtime, I should think. Would you like
                to leave a – well, who shall I say called, then?
                Hello . . . hello!

                (*The caller has rung off. She replaces the phone
                and dusts it casually, then picks up the
                typewriter and moves it to the window-ledge,
                where it joins a miscellaneous pile of scripts and
                files. Returning to the desk, she dusts it until her
                attention is caught by a pile of letters, which she
                picks up and scans through rapidly. The rattle of
                a key in the lock makes her drop them and leave
                the desk hurriedly. She is dusting furniture,
                humming a popular hit to herself, as the door
                opens and* KAREN *enters, carrying a bunch of
                yellow chrysanthemums. This is a changed* KAREN,
                *erect and confident, as though completely
                recovered from her recent ordeal.*)

STELLA   Hello, ~~madam~~! I wasn't expecting you back so
                soon.

KAREN   I can't stand Kingsmead on a market day –
                nowhere to park and the whole place packed to
                suffocation. Get me some water for these, would
                you?

STELLA   ~~Yes, madam~~. Sure (*She takes a vase off L as* KAREN *gets
                scissors from a desk drawer to snip the stems.*
                STELLA *returns.*)

KAREN   Thank you, Stella. I'll see to them, you carry on.

         (STELLA *works industriously as* KAREN *arranges the flowers.*)

KAREN   Any messages?

STELLA   A man ~~called, asking for you~~ came round. He went away when I told him you were out but I think he's coming back.

KAREN   Did he leave his name?

STELLA   Davies. (*The scissors clatter to the desk.*)

STELLA   (*concerned*) Madam!

KAREN   It's nothing – I jabbed my finger on the scissors.

STELLA   ~~Shall I get a dressing?~~ Do you need a plaster

KAREN   No, it isn't even bleeding. Are you sure this man said "Davies"?

STELLA   That's what it sounded like. I couldn't be certain though because he spoke like a foreigner – Yorkshire, I think.

KAREN   I see. Oh, bother! I meant to post these letters in the village – it slipped my mind.

STELLA   I'll take 'em down if you like, soon as I've got the lunch on.

KAREN   If you can spare the time: some of them are rather urgent. (*Door buzzer.*)

STELLA   That'll be him now, I expect. (KAREN *positions the vase as* STELLA *answers the door and after a word of conversation, looks round at her.*)

STELLA   It's Miss Cunningham, madam.

KAREN   (*the name is unfamiliar*) Who?

STELLA   Miss –

KAREN   Ask her to come in.

STELLA   (*to someone, off*) Would you like to come in?

               (MISS CUNNINGHAM *enters, a middle-aged woman
               in tweeds and a neat hat. Her innate shrewdness
               is not immediately apparent, beneath the surface
               "gush". She carries a shopping basket
               containing her library books.*)

MISS C   (*as she comes*) Thank you so much.

STELLA   (*closes door*) Don't mention it. (MISS CUNNINGHAM
               looks at her askance. STELLA *remembers her
               place.*)

STELLA   'Scuse me. (*She dodges in front of the visitor and
               takes her cloths out L.*)

KAREN   What can I do for you, Miss . . .

MISS C   Cunningham. Eleanor Cunningham, your next door
               neighbour – well, nearly but not quite! You may
               have noticed my little pink bungalow up the road
               . . . (*Preens.*) . . . "The Nook"?

KAREN   Of course; it's charming. Do sit down.

MISS C   Thank you. (*Settles.*)

KAREN   Can I get some coffee?

MISS C   Not for me, thank you – ~~I'm on a diet.~~ I've only got a few minutes Besides,
               I've only got a few minutes – I'm waiting for my
               bus down to the library and couldn't resist the
               opportunity of popping in to introduce myself.

KAREN   I'm glad you thought of it.

MISS C   I've looked forward to meeting you for so long but somehow I've always missed you on your previous visits.

KAREN   I'm not here very often.

MISS C   This time I was quite determined . . . particularly since you appear to be staying on for a little while?

KAREN   Only long enough for my husband to finish his new book, I'm afraid.

MISS C   Oh, don't say that! I was so hoping I could interest you in one or two of our local activities. We're such a busy little community, you know – I'm chairman of the Women's Guild over at St Chad's . . . (*Leans forward confidentially.*) Seven hundred and fifty [*thousand*] pounds we've raised for charity in less than four years and the annual subscription's only ~~fifty pence~~ [£5].

KAREN   (*takes the hint*) I'd love to be a member even though I can't be of much assistance – apart from the subscription, of course.

MISS C   (*beams*) Oh, would you! Would you really?

KAREN   (*to handbag*) ~~Fifty pence~~ [£5], I think you said?

MISS C   That's the minimum, of course. (*Takes out receipt book.*) I'll make out your receipt – you see I came fully prepared. Now, where's my pen? (*Hunts.*) I'd have cast my net for you earlier in the week but I've been in town for the last few days, visiting my brother.

KAREN   (*brings coin*) There you are.

MISS C   (*not impressed*) ~~Fifty pence~~ [£5]. (*Turns on the charm.*) Thank you so much! We ought to have you in the Dramatic Society, with a figure like yours. But there – if you're only going to be here today and gone tomorrow – they rehearse, you see, for three

months at least. (*Writes.*) Fifty pence. (*Signs.*)
Your receipt, my dear – the membership card will
follow ~~through~~ the post.
in

KAREN   Thank you.

MISS C   Such a pity you won't be with us in the winter –
there's so much going on then, the summer's quite
dead by comparison.

KAREN   My husband says the place attracts a lot of
summer visitors.

MISS C   Mostly of the wrong sort, I'm afraid. Sometimes
it's quite unbearable. On fine summer evenings the
whole place breaks out in a rash of sports cars and
courting couples. That little beech copse over the
road now, that's quite a favourite spot.

KAREN   It's a lovely view from there.

MISS C   Not at midnight. That's their peak period. It's
positively maddening to have one's rest disturbed
time and again by powerful engines starting up
and roaring off into the night.

KAREN   I can't say I've noticed much noise.

MISS C   You will, my dear, you will. There's one little red
car in particular – it's round here most weekends –
but surely you noticed it last Friday night when
you had your little upset? It was parked under the
trees across the way.

KAREN   Are you sure?

MISS C   I saw it with my own eyes.

KAREN   What time was this?

MISS C   The time the crash occurred. It woke me up and
trembling like a leaf, I flew to the window. It was
then I picked out this other car, lurking in the
shadows.

KAREN   Was anyone in it?

MISS C   I'm not sure. I was so overwrought I had to go and make a pot of tea.

KAREN   How long had it been there, do you know?

MISS C   I've no idea: I'd gone to bed early that evening to make sure of being up in time for the first train to London. I sleep so badly –

KAREN   And did you see it go?

MISS C   No – but it left soon afterwards, of that I'm certain.

KAREN   Why?

MISS C   I took my cup of tea to the window a little later on and the red car had gone, vanished into thin air. It can't have gone past The Nook or I'd have heard it – you couldn't miss that engine. (STELLA *enters, in her coat.*)

STELLA   I'm sorry, madam – lunch is on and it's nearly half past twelve. If you want me to take the letters –

MISS C   (*rises*) Half-twelve? I must fly.

KAREN   (*gets letters*) Must you go?

MISS C   I'm afraid so, I've a million things to do – but I'll give you a tinkle soon, if I may?

KAREN   Please do. Come and have tea, I'd like you to meet my husband.

MISS C   I'd be thrilled – he's quite the local celebrity. Goodbye, Mrs Holt – thank you so much.

STELLA   Here's the bus, madam.

KAREN   Oh. (*Hands letters.*) Don't be long, Stella.

MISS C   (*in doorway*) Are you taking it too? How
            splendid, you can carry my basket. (*Dumps it on
            her.*) Bye bye! (*She sails out.* STELLA *turns to*
            KAREN *in indignation.*)

STELLA   Well, some people!

            (*She follows.* KAREN *thinks for a moment, still
            looking at the door. Then she moves to the
            telephone and almost picks it up, then decides
            against it. She takes the tissue paper the flowers
            have been wrapped in from the desk, screws it up
            in a ball and drops it in the wastepaper basket.
            Then she comes back to the phone and picks it
            up, decisively.*)

KAREN   Kingsmead two-six, please. (*Pause as she glances
            at her watch.*) Hello – Lightowlers? This is Mrs
            Holt. Can you tell me if my husband's in the shop?
            Oh, he must have gone. You mean he hasn't been
            in at all this morning? I understood he was coming
            down specially for some typewriter ribbons, and I
            believe he wanted to see you about some
            duplicating work. He probably changed his plans.
            No, no, he'll be in touch with you soon. I'm sure
            you will. (*Door buzzer.*)

KAREN   Excuse me, I must go. Goodbye. (*She hangs up
            and goes to the door.*)

DAVIES   (*off*) Morning, Mrs Holt!

KAREN   Inspector – do come in.

DAVIES   Thank you. (*Enters.*) I hope it's not inconvenient?

KAREN   Not at all, I'm delighted to see you again. (*He
            spots the flowers as he puts his hat down.*)

DAVIES   My word, what lovely chrysanths! Grew – 'em
            yourself, did you?

KAREN   Unfortunately, no – I haven't your talent for gardening.

DAVIES   Oh, I'm not much of a gardener. I always say my job's digging things up, not making 'em grow.

KAREN   Most appropriate. You came before, I believe?

DAVIES   Yes. I happened to be in the district and thought I might as well drop in and see how you were getting on.

KAREN   I see. (*Relieved.*) A purely social visit?

DAVIES   You might call it that.

KAREN   Sit down, won't you?

DAVIES   Just for a minute. (*Sits.*) I've been talking to Will Purdie at the garage. He tells me you've got your car back.

KAREN   Yes, he's done it very well – you can't see a scratch.

DAVIES   Aye, he knows his job, does Will. How's your husband keeping?

KAREN   He's fine.

DAVIES   I was hoping to catch him in this time.

KAREN   He'll be back for lunch. Was it – anything in particular?

DAVIES   No, not really. Just one or two things I want to ask him about last Friday night.

KAREN   The night of the accident?

DAVIES   That's right. He was out at the time, wasn't he?

KAREN   Yes, he'd gone for a stroll a few minutes before I arrived.

DAVIES   Funny time of night to do that.

KAREN   Writers are pretty unpredictable. There's nothing
           Howard likes better than a walk when he's got
           something on his mind.

DAVIES   (*easily*) Such as what?

KAREN   Problems connected with his work. When he's
           writing he lives in a world of his own. I never even
           know what he's working on until he gives me the
           final script.

DAVIES   For criticism – or approval?

KAREN   For consideration. I'm his publisher.

DAVIES   That's useful! (*Rises.*) He didn't happen to
           mention whether he'd noticed any strangers
           hanging about that evening?

KAREN   While he was out? Prowlers, do you mean?

DAVIES   Not necessarily. Anything or anyone at all
           unusual.

KAREN   He didn't say so.

DAVIES   You recollect telling me, Mrs Holt, that as far as
           you knew there were no witnesses?

KAREN   I do.

DAVIES   In other words, you didn't see anybody yourself
           when you got out of the car?

KAREN   Not a soul.

DAVIES   You're sure?

KAREN   I couldn't be absolutely sure, it was a very dark
           night. What's all this leading up to, Inspector?

DAVIES   According to our information, shortly before ten
          o'clock that night a small red sports car was
          parked over the road there, without lights. You
          didn't notice it?

KAREN   Wait – I believe I do remember something. It was
          only a glimpse as I turned the corner. There was
          someone in it, I think.

DAVIES   Who?

KAREN   A man and a woman. I couldn't be positive, I only
          saw them for a moment.

DAVIES   So it's no use asking for a description?

KAREN   I'm afraid not.

DAVIES   Pity.

KAREN   What makes you so interested in this car?

DAVIES   It's not so much the car we're interested in, as the
          owner.

KAREN   Why?

DAVIES   I think I told you there's been a spot of mischief
          over at the Grange – burglary.

KAREN   Yes, I read all about it in the local paper.

DAVIES   Well, whoever was responsible for that had the
          use of a car, and the Grange isn't too far away
          from here.

KAREN   Why do you think it was this particular one?

DAVIES   We don't, we're simply making a few general
          inquiries. But it's been spotted in these parts
          before, usually at weekends – Tom Briggs has
          seen it more than once. We'd like to find out who
          it belongs to and what they were doing here last
          Friday night.

KAREN   Here?

DAVIES   Well, hereabouts. You didn't get the number, by
          any chance?

KAREN   How could I? It was so dark

DAVIES   I just thought in the circumstances you might
          have gone across for help.

KAREN   There was nothing they could do. My one thought
          was to rush in here and telephone the police.
          When I went out again the car had vanished.

DAVIES   (*keenly*) When you went out again?

KAREN   (*easily*) To adjust the headlights.

DAVIES   Ah yes – I was forgetting. And you're quite sure
          it had gone?

KAREN   ~~I made a note of it.~~ Yes

DAVIES   Mrs Holt, doesn't it seem strange to you that after
          making a note of the movements of this car, you
          should have forgotten all about seeing it until I
          brought the matter up?

KAREN   That's easily explained. It seemed so odd that it
          should vanish like that. I wondered if I'd really
          seen it at all in the first place! As it was, I
          dismissed it as a trick of the light.

DAVIES   That's feasible enough – except there wasn't any
          light. The street lamp was out.

KAREN   There must have been a moon.

DAVIES   Not that night, according to my diary. You said
          yourself how dark it was. (*Sits.*) Now let's try and
          get this straight, shall we? You took a left-hand
          bend travelling fast with your headlights dipped.
          Then you turned in left, sharp left, to enter this

drive of yours. However did you manage to spot a
small two-seater parked in pitch-blackness on your
right? (*Pause.*) Eh, Mrs Holt?

KAREN   Inspector, I'm not fond of cross-examinations.

DAVIES   (*immediately jocular*) Oh, this is nothing like that!
It's just a friendly little chat. But, in your own
interests –

KAREN   In my own interests – I'm not going to be drawn
into a discussion. It's almost a week ago now, and –

DAVIES   Now Mrs Holt, there's no need to act upset. I'm
only trying to sort things out. We know the car
was here that night, we know what time it arrived
and we've a pretty shrewd idea of who was driving
it.

KAREN   (*stiffens*) Oh?

DAVIES   A young woman – ~~redhead~~, she stopped at
Purdie's place for cigarettes, Will remembers her
quite well. Soon after that, Mrs Purdie went past
here on her bike, and saw the car parked just
across the way. That was shortly before you came
on the scene.

KAREN   Inspector, I'm not really concerned in all this –
why are you telling me?

DAVIES   We're anxious to find the girl and ask her a few
questions, that's all.

KAREN   But how am I supposed to help?

DAVIES   The events are pretty close, you must admit. And
when you said you saw two people in the car –

KAREN   I said I wasn't sure. But isn't it obvious? This girl
came up here to meet a boyfriend. You'll find
couples over there any night of the week. My
guess is they sat together in the car and after

seeing me have my smash they left as quickly as possible to avoid being dragged in as witnesses.

DAVIES   Why on earth should they do that?

KAREN   Because they didn't want to be involved. You know what people are. There might be a dozen reasons. Perhaps one of them was married.

DAVIES   (*twinkles*) Do you know, I never thought of that.

KAREN   You should. It happens more often than you think.

DAVIES   That's what comes of having a settled family life, you drop out of touch with these modern habits. That would account for it, certainly . . . except for one small snag. When Mrs Purdie went past, the car was empty.

KAREN   Those woods are very popular for evening strolls.

DAVIES   It can't have been a very long stroll if they were back by the time you showed up. That was at ten o'clock, remember, and the girl couldn't have got here much before ten-to. How do we account for that?

KAREN   (*lightly*) It's not my place to account for anything. You're supposed to do the theorising – isn't that what you're paid for?

DAVIES   Partly – though I'm not very good at it.

KAREN   Then take my tip, Inspector, and look elsewhere for your criminals. Nowadays young, attractive girls don't have to resort to burglary to make a living.

DAVIES   (*reaches for hat*) No – but you'd be surprised what some of 'em *do* get up to. (HOWARD *enters by the front door.*)

HOWARD   Darling, I'm so sorry – hello, Inspector! What are you doing here?

DAVIES   Just paying a social call.

KAREN   Inspector Davies wanted to ask a few questions,
                Howard.

HOWARD   Really? What sort of questions?

DAVIES   I'll leave it to your wife to explain if you don't
                mind. I must be off.

KAREN   I thought you wanted to talk to Howard?

DAVIES   No, no, that won't be necessary now. Goodbye,
                Mrs Holt, thanks for your help.

KAREN   I've done nothing.

DAVIES   On the contrary. You've done more than I
                expected. (*Affably.*) I'll see you again. (*He nods at
                them both, and leaves.*)

HOWARD   What sort of questions?

KAREN   The right questions. Unfortunately, I couldn't
                supply the right answers.

HOWARD   ~~Tell me.~~ What do you mean?

KAREN   (*moves away*) What makes a man like that become
                a detective, do you suppose? The inquiring mind –
                a sense of duty – or a nasty little quirk of
                character that makes him enjoy seeing other
                people suffer?

HOWARD   *What sort of questions?*

KAREN   (*faces him*) Why didn't you tell me about the car,
                Howard? You should have done . . . it might have
                helped.

HOWARD   Car?

KAREN   The red sports car that was here that night. A
                young girl drove it up. She's wanted by the police.

HOWARD   What!

KAREN   Don't be alarmed, they don't know what's become
           of her – yet. They think she's mixed up in this
           business at the Grange. But we know differently,
           don't we, Howard? Now do you see why I couldn't
           give the right answers without putting a rope
           round our necks?   *without dropping us in it.*

HOWARD   Hadn't you better start at the beginning?

KAREN   (*flatly*) Inspector Davies wants to know what that
           car was doing here – he wants to interview the
           owner.

HOWARD   I don't know anything about it.

KAREN   I do, Howard – I saw it. What's more, I told him
           so.

           (*He swings round angrily.*)

KAREN   What I didn't tell him was the car left here at nine
           minutes past ten and drove off down the hill. I
           heard it go and checked the time. You must have
           heard it too, and seen it, but you never mentioned
           it – why, Howard? Because you couldn't. Because
           when that car left here that night you were driving
           it.

HOWARD   (*defiantly*) What if I was? I had to get the girl
           away quickly.

KAREN   You must have known it was hers.

HOWARD   I guessed.

KAREN   You guessed nothing. You knew, because you
           knew her – *intimately*.

HOWARD   Karen, listen to me –

KAREN   You can't tell me anything I don't already know. I
           found my picture hidden in a drawer, her lipstick

on a cigarette – a ~~brand we never use. I pick~~ up a
magazine and smell her ~~perfume – I~~ can smell it
still, ~~drifting on the air,~~ only now it's mixed up
~~with the scent of death.~~ She was here with you
that night and *other* nights. Wasn't she? (*He
cannot reply.*)

KAREN   (*blazes*) Answer me!

HOWARD   What for? (*Turns.*) You know the answer. (KAREN
*sways as if she's been struck. She feels for a
chair.*)

KAREN   That's why you were so ready to take care of
everything for me . . . because it covered up
everything – for you. (*Pause.*)

HOWARD   How much of this did you tell Davies?

KAREN   Only that I saw the car. What else could I tell him?

     (*He watches her for a moment, as she sits, empty
and disillusioned; then he goes behind her.*)

HOWARD   I'm glad it's out, at last. (*Hands gently on her
shoulders.*) Karen, darling, if only you'd let me –

KAREN   (*frozen*) It isn't any use, Howard. (*His hands fall
to his sides.*)

KAREN   It wasn't the best of marriages but I did what I
could to make it . . . happy. In spite of all your
debts, the quarrels about money, the awful . . .
uncertainty. But after this – (*Her head falls. He
comes round and kneels beside her.*)

     Karen I love you I'll never let anything

HOWARD   ~~Let me ask you something~~ – do you honestly think
like you ~~it could ever~~ happen – again? (*She looks at him.*)
~~No, Karen.~~

KAREN   It's so easy to say, isn't it?

HOWARD   I'm to blame for everything, I admit that. (*Rises
and breaks away.*) Everything. Her name was

Julie, Julie Grant. I'd known her the best part of a
year. She was ~~very~~ young, very lovely . . . and you
killed her. (*Turns to her.*) Don't you see now why
it had to be hushed up, for both our sakes?

KAREN   No, Howard. I don't.

HOWARD   We were lovers. Would that make things any
better if the police found out? (*She catches her
breath.*)

HOWARD   Or wouldn't it supply – a motive?

KAREN   (*softly*) Thank God they don't suspect the truth.

HOWARD   They don't – but someone does. (*He takes an
envelope from his pocket, extracts a letter and
holds it out.*) Read it. (*She does so, slowly, then
looks up at him, horror-stricken.*)

KAREN   When did you get this?

HOWARD   This morning. Through the post.

KAREN   Why didn't you tell me?

HOWARD   Believe it or not I wanted to spare your feelings.
That's why I went out. I've been walking in the
woods, wondering how to fight it. Blackmail's
something new to me.

KAREN   It's – horrible. (*He takes the sheet back.*)

HOWARD   "Unless you want the police to know about Friday,
twenty have ~~two~~ thousand pounds ready in cash and
await instructions."

KAREN   (*rises*) I think I half expected this from the
beginning. It's what I've always been afraid of –
that someone saw. But who . . . who?

HOWARD   Disguised handwriting – cheap notepaper posted
in London. What do we do now?

KAREN   Pay.

HOWARD   We can't let them get away with this!

KAREN   What else – call in the inspector? "I'm sorry, Mr
            Davies, there's been another complication. We're
            being blackmailed because I killed a girl and my
            husband disposed of the body. Would you kindly
            look into it?" He'd be only too delighted.

HOWARD   If we could get to know how much they saw –

KAREN   That'll come. They'll tell us, bit by bit, as the price
            goes up.

HOWARD   There must be some way of finding out.

KAREN   It'll take time.

HOWARD   Meanwhile – we pay?

KAREN   We pay until it hurts. (*Door buzzer.* HOWARD
            answers it. KAREN *sits again.* HOWARD *admits*
            STELLA, *the maid.*)

STELLA   Thank you, ~~sir~~. I'm sorry, the back door's locked.

KAREN   You've been a long time.

STELLA   Miss Cunningham kept me talking, ~~madam~~ – things
            that woman asked!

KAREN   You'd better see to lunch. (STELLA *goes L, then
            turns.*)

STELLA   (*with a smile*) Oh. Before I forget, ~~sir~~ – there was a
            phone call for you while you were out.

HOWARD   Who was it?

STELLA   A gentleman. He said he'd ring you back.

HOWARD   Did he give his name?

STELLA   ~~No, sir.~~ I asked him to but he rang off. (*Smirks.*) *a smile* Perhaps it was ~~long-distance and he wanted to dodge the pips~~.

~~HOWARD~~   (*looks at her, shrewdly*) ~~How clever of you to think of that.~~

~~STELLA~~   ~~Sir?~~

KAREN   That'll be all, Stella.

STELLA   ~~Yes, madam.~~ (*She goes out L.*)

HOWARD   Sure we can trust her?

KAREN   Howard, you can't suspect –

HOWARD   Maybe, maybe not. It could be anyone. (*Sits by her.*) Scared, Karen?

KAREN   Aren't you?

HOWARD   Yes . . . but grateful, too. If we've got to face this thing at all I'm grateful that we're facing it together. (*He looks at her, almost pleadingly. She puts her hand on his. The telephone rings, stridently.* HOWARD *looks round at it, then back to* KAREN. *Both are afraid. He rises to answer it.*)

HOWARD   Yes? (*Waits.*) ~~Put them through.~~ (*Looks at* KAREN.) ~~Long-distance.~~ (*He holds her gaze for a moment then breaks it as he specks into the phone.*) Speaking. Good morning – we've been waiting for you.

         (*Blackout.*)

Scene Two

The same. Some weeks later. It is late and HOWARD *sits alone at the desk, writing a letter. The bedroom door opens and* STELLA *comes out with an empty glass on a tray.* HOWARD *closes a side-leaf of the blotter over his letter and rises.*

HOWARD	How is she?
STELLA	(*closes door*) ~~Madam~~ She's asleep.
HOWARD	Did the doctor come?
STELLA	Yes ~~sir,~~ just after lunch. He gave her a sedative. I'm not sure which but I think it was the strong one.
HOWARD	(*concerned*) Did he seem satisfied?
STELLA	Oh, yes! Don't you worry, ~~Mrs Holt~~ she's going to be ~~allright.~~ fine.
HOWARD	I hope so.
STELLA	If you don't mind, ~~sir,~~ I'll be going soon. ~~Madam~~ Mrs Hesslt said I could leave early today.
HOWARD	Certainly. Got a date?
STELLA	Only the pictures, with my sister.
HOWARD	Haven't you got a boyfriend?
STELLA	Yes – but he's ~~down south,~~ away working, ~~learning how~~ to be a chef. He only comes up at weekends.
HOWARD	I see. (*A thought strikes him.*) Does he – (*Stops.*)
STELLA	~~Sir?~~ Yes?
HOWARD	(*steadily*) Does he come to Kingsmead every weekend?
STELLA	More often than not, although – (*Door buzzer.*) Excuse me. (*She puts down her tray and goes to the door.* MISS CUNNINGHAM *thrusts on, bearing a small bunch of flowers.*)
STELLA	It's Miss –

MISS C	My dear Mr Holt!
HOWARD	Miss Cunningham, what a pleasant surprise. (*It isn't.*)
MISS C	I'm on my way to a committee meeting and felt I couldn't pass the door without calling in to say hello. (STELLA *closes the door and retrieves her tray.*)
HOWARD	Won't you sit down?
MISS C	Thank you so much. (*Settles.*)
STELLA	I'll leave you to it then, ~~sir~~.
HOWARD	All right, Stella, ~~run along~~, enjoy the film.
STELLA	Thank you, ~~sir~~. Bye bye – (*At* MISS C.) – both. (*She goes.*)
MISS C	I do hope you're keeping a weather eye on that girl.
HOWARD	Why do you say that?
MISS C	The family have such a bad name down in the village.
HOWARD	All I know is she's a jolly hard worker. Since my wife's illness she's been a tremendous help.
MISS C	That's what I really came about. How is dear Mrs Holt?
HOWARD	Much better, thank you.
MISS C	I'm so glad. I brought these along from my garden – they're specially picked.
HOWARD	Very good of you.
MISS C	(*rises*) I wonder if I might take them in to her?

HOWARD   I'll do that later, if you don't mind. She's sound
            asleep – doctor's orders.

MISS C   Then I shouldn't dream of disturbing her. (*Gives
            them to him.*) Rest is the great healer.

HOWARD   Especially ~~in these nervous disorders.~~ with stress

MISS C   (*sits again*) Strange, isn't it, that Mrs Holt could
            suffer from ~~her nerves~~? She's always seemed so
            calm, so self-controlled.   stress

HOWARD   Underneath, she's highly sensitive – and I don't
            believe she's altogether shaken off the effects of
            her accident, some weeks ago.

MISS C   (*interested*) Oh? I don't believe I heard about that.

HOWARD   But surely – she discussed it with you.

MISS C   No, no. That was your accident we talked about.

            (*A moment.*)

HOWARD   (*carefully*) My accident?

MISS C   The night you collided with the street lamp.

HOWARD   There must be some mistake, Miss Cunningham.

MISS C   But I remember most distinctly. I was at the
            window within seconds of the crash and I watched
            you climb out of the driving seat.

HOWARD   That was my wife you saw.

MISS C   There's nothing wrong with my eyes, Mr Holt –
            though I do get the most dreadful sinus headaches
            sometimes.

HOWARD   Would you mind telling me exactly what you saw
            that night?

MISS C	You were wearing a light-coloured ~~raincoat and no hat~~ *jacket* – I picked you out as you passed through the glare of the headlights.
HOWARD	How observant of you! Have you told anyone else?
MISS C	I don't think so. I tried to talk it over with your wife a couple of times but the mere mention of the incident so distressed her I thought, "Better leave well alone."
HOWARD	You're sure no one else knows?
MISS C	Oh, quite! Is it so ~~dreadful~~ly important?
HOWARD	Yes, I'm afraid it is. (*Sits near her.*) Miss Cunningham, you're a very understanding person; I'm going to take you into my confidence.
MISS C	Well, if you really feel –
HOWARD	You're perfectly right in all you saw that night. The whole thing was my fault but my wife very kindly agreed to take the responsibility.
MISS C	But why?
HOWARD	It was a question of insurance. (*Smiles.*) You see, I'm not a very good driver, I'm afraid.
MISS C	I always knew we had a lot in common – I've failed the test three times!
HOWARD	As it was simply a case of damage, to the vehicle . . . no one was hurt, of course, you knew that?
MISS C	I've been under that impression.
HOWARD	To be frank, the car's insured in my wife's name and – (*Smiles disarmingly.*) – need I say more?
MISS C	I understand perfectly.

HOWARD   And you don't blame me?

MISS C   Not in the least! I'm all for doing the authorities in
            the eye whenever we get the chance.

HOWARD   One must try and preserve one's sense of
            independence.

MISS C   My feeling exactly! It's the only way to save this
            country from out-and-out bureaucracy.

HOWARD   Tell me, as a matter of interest, what else did you
            witness that night?

MISS C   Nothing exciting. After the crash I went to make
            some tea and when I came back all I could see was
            Sergeant Briggs poking about at the scene of the
            crime.

HOWARD   Crime?

MISS C   Speaking *figuratively*, of course. Now I refuse to
            discuss it further – the incident is closed.

HOWARD   I appreciate your cooperation.

MISS C   (*opens it again*) There's only one thing puzzles
            me. You tell me Mrs Holt is suffering from the after
            effects but surely, if you were the one involved –

HOWARD   As I said, Karen's very highly strung. The mere
            thought of doing anything dishonest is enough to
            upset her, and to make matters worse the police
            have been here several times about this business
            at the Grange.

MISS C   My dear boy, they've called on everyone.

HOWARD   (*surprised*) Even you?

MISS C   Yes, I had a long talk with Tom Briggs. Charming
            man, what a pity he's a policeman. He told me they
            were interviewing everyone in the district.

HOWARD	Did he mention us at all?
MISS C	Not ~~personally~~. Why? *specifically*
HOWARD	I'm not sure the inspector entirely believed our version of the accident.
MISS C	Oh, I don't think the police have any worries on that score.
HOWARD	Nevertheless, in view of our little charade with the insurance company, it's rather disturbing. If anyone should take into their heads to question you about it . . .
MISS C	You may safely leave them to me. (*Rises.*) Now I must go, or I shall miss the minutes. You won't forget the flowers for Mrs Holt?
HOWARD	I'll put them in water immediately. Thank you again . . . from both of us.
MISS C	~~Rubbish~~ – anything at all I can do . . . but you will bear in mind you've promised to attend one of our Social Evenings shortly? *It's my pleasure*
HOWARD	As soon as my wife's well again.
MISS C	One good turn deserves another. (*She smiles down at her gloves as she draws them on.*)
HOWARD	That sounds like gentle blackmail. I shouldn't have thought you were the type.
MISS C	You'd be surprised what I can stoop to, on occasion.
HOWARD	I'd better be on my guard.
MISS C	I shouldn't let it bother you. (*Looks up at him.*) I'm confident you can cope most readily with any little demands I have to make. (*Telephone rings.*) There, now! Don't trouble to see me out, it may be urgent. I'll pop in later in the week. Goodbye!

(*She waves once and is gone. He stares after her
with a worried frown. The phone rings
persistently. He dumps the flowers in the
wastepaper basket and goes to it.*)

HOWARD   (*into phone*) Hello? Terry! I asked you not to use
this number. I know – I haven't been able to get to
town lately. Things have been damned difficult
these last few weeks – Karen and I, we've had a
lot of . . . unforeseen expenses. Of course you'll
get it – I promised, didn't I? No. I can't say when.
Don't be a fool, you mustn't do that Terry! (*Works
receiver hook.*) Oh, I thought we'd been cut off.
All right – this weekend if possible – I'll do what I
can. (*He hangs up impatiently, then looks round
the room and to the bedroom. Door buzzer. He
answers it.*)

DAVIES   (*off, amiable*) Hello, sir. Mind if I come in?

HOWARD   (*stands back*) I thought you'd finished with us?

DAVIES   (*enters*) No, not quite. Warm, for the time of year?

HOWARD   ~~I suppose it is.~~

DAVIES   (*hat down*) ~~This'll teach me to take my holidays in
May!~~

HOWARD   Inspector, you didn't come here to talk about the
weather.

DAVIES   (*laughs*) Not primarily, no. Is your wife in?

HOWARD   (*door in hand*) ~~Mrs Holt~~ Shot 's ill in bed.

DAVIES   Oh, I am sorry. What's the ~~trouble~~? Matter with her?

HOWARD   ~~Nervous strain~~. Stress

DAVIES   Been worrying too much, has she?

HOWARD   I'm afraid I can't let you see her.

DAVIES That's understandable. I'll call again. (HOWARD *closes the door and stands against it.*)

HOWARD What's the trouble, Inspector?

DAVIES It'll keep, Mr Holt.

HOWARD That's not what I asked. Still chasing burglars?

DAVIES Not any more. That case is closed. I'll be going back to Chelmsford in a couple of days.

HOWARD We'll be quite sorry to lose you.

DAVIES (*grins*) Nice of you.

✗ HOWARD Who did it?

DAVIES Two young lads in the village – window cleaners, as a matter of fact. They found a new use for the ladders. But they made their mistake in trying to dispose of the stuff locally and we nabbed 'em.

HOWARD Congratulations.

DAVIES Oh, it wasn't much of a job, bit on the dull side. I don't care for amateurs, Mr Holt. If ever you decide to go in for crime, don't dabble, do the job properly. Crime doesn't pay – unless you're a professional.

HOWARD I'll bear that in mind. ~~Cigarette~~?

DAVIES ~~No thanks, I've got my pipe~~.

✓ HOWARD If you've finished here, why d'you want to see ~~Mrs Holt~~? my wife

DAVIES Funny how one thing leads to another. I've got a different sort of problem on my hands now and I thought she might be able to help us on a little matter of identification. (*He takes a postcard photograph from his wallet.*)

HOWARD	Anything I can do?
DAVIES	I don't think so, thanks all the same. (*Starts to return it.*)
HOWARD	I know most of my wife's friends.
DAVIES	You wouldn't call this a friend, exactly.
HOWARD	May I see?
DAVIES	If you like. (*Passes it over.*)
HOWARD	(*studies it*) Who's it supposed to be?
DAVIES	A girl called Julie Grant. (HOWARD *looks up.*)
DAVIES	Does that ring a bell?
HOWARD	How extraordinary. It's a name I used once in a book of mine. (*Tries to hand it hack.*)
DAVIES	Which book was that, Mr Holt?
HOWARD	(*smoothly*) It's been out of print for years.
DAVIES	I see. (*Takes it.*) And you've never met this girl?
HOWARD	Certainly not. I'm sure that goes for my wife, too. What's she supposed to have done?
DAVIES	She hasn't done anything. It's what's been done to her that concerns us. She's been reported missing.
HOWARD	Really?
DAVIES	(*proffers it again*) You're sure you've never seen her?
HOWARD	I shouldn't be likely to forget it if I had. She's most attractive.

DAVIES   Yes, she's a bonny lass, is our Julie – or was.

HOWARD   Was?

DAVIES   (*looks at him*) That's what we're trying to
          establish. We've found out quite a bit about her,
          thanks to her landlady. She had a little furnished
          flat in London, near Victoria Station.

HOWARD   Is she a London girl?

DAVIES   No, she went there from the Midlands soon after
          she left school. Took a job as a waitress but that
          wasn't good enough for her so she decided to go
          in for modelling – ladies' fashions, all that sort of
          thing. She scraped enough together for a course
          of training and made quite a success of it . . . it got
          her a job with Victor Heath, anyway, in Bruton
          Street, Mayfair.

HOWARD   Good firm – Karen goes there sometimes.

DAVIES   Too good, for this girl. She got a bit above herself
          and had to leave without a reference. After that
          she drifted for a while and then, according to Mrs
          Ramsay, she hit the jackpot – found herself a rich
          boyfriend who was more or less permanent. He did
          a lot for Julie. She even ran her own little car.
          Sports model. Red.   little red flashy thing...

HOWARD   Now I'm beginning to see daylight. My wife said
          you'd been making inquiries about something of
          the sort.

DAVIES   Julie left London in it on the night of September
          the fourth and she hasn't been seen since.

HOWARD   And you have reason to believe she's living
          somewhere in these parts?

DAVIES   Nothing concrete, as yet. We've got the number of
          the car and we're trying to link it up with one or
          two bits of local evidence. If we could find out
          what's become of that car it would be something.

HOWARD　　Missing cars, I take it, are easier to trace than missing persons?

DAVIES　　At least we've got licence plates and registration books to help us. With people there's no telling where they'll go or what they'll do.

(handwritten annotation: the registration no → DVLA)

HOWARD　　I read somewhere that eight thousand people vanish every year without trace, and nearly all the disappearances are voluntary.

DAVIES　　That's true – in most cases we're powerless to act. You can't call in the CID every time a fellow leaves his wife – unless he's cut her throat first.

HOWARD　　But you don't suspect anything like that in this instance?

DAVIES　　That remains to be seen, doesn't it? We're always ready to take action if someone disappears in suspicious circumstances. (*Slight pause.*) This girl was pregnant.

HOWARD　　How do you know?

DAVIES　　The landlady told us.

HOWARD　　So Mrs Ramsay reported her missing?

DAVIES　　(*stares*) Mrs Ramsay?

HOWARD　　The landlady – didn't you say that was her name?

DAVIES　　Did I? (*Relaxes.*) Yes, perhaps I did. But Mrs Ramsay wasn't worried – the girl often went off on her own, for quite long spells and the rent was always up-to-date. That's all landladies seem to care about, nowadays. In fact a further instalment arrived a fortnight after September the fourth, by post.

HOWARD　　Was that remarkable?

DAVIES   No, not especially – except this time it came in a
            registered envelope and the address was typed.
            That was new.

HOWARD   But hardly new enough to start an investigation.

DAVIES   Granted. Mrs Ramsay bunged it in the bank and
            never gave it a second thought.

HOWARD   Then why did she report the girl missing?

DAVIES   She didn't. That was someone else. Someone else
            entirely.

HOWARD   Who?

DAVIES   The girl's father.

            (*This comes as something of a shock and* HOWARD
            can't help showing it slightly.)

DAVIES   Didn't I mention him? That's not surprising, he's
            been kept in the background for a long time now.
            Julie never talked about him – it came as quite an
            eye-opener to Mrs Ramsay to find the girl wasn't
            all alone in the world. He's a drunk, a lay-about,
            who lives from one pub to the next. Julie sent him
            money every month, on condition that he never
            tried to see her – to save embarrassment, I
            suppose, in front of her posh friends. So he
            stayed well away in case his little source of
            income might suddenly dry up. But that's what
            happened in the middle of September, for no good
            reason at all that he can think of. He's had no
            word from her since – and precious little to drink!
            So he got in touch with us, and that's what started
            the ball rolling. (HOWARD *goes to pour a drink.*)

DAVIES   Odd little story, isn't it?

HOWARD   Fascinating.

DAVIES   I thought you might be interested.

HOWARD   You said something just now about local evidence.

DAVIES   Oh, yes. We have reason to believe Julie was seen in Kingsmead on the night she disappeared. A young woman answering to her description *pack* bought a ~~box~~ of cigarettes at Purdie's Garage. ~~Fifty Grenville, cork-tipped~~. I've shown the photograph to Will and he knew her straightaway. As far as we can make out that was her last recorded appearance.

HOWARD   (*carefully*) How did you get on to all this?

DAVIES   The photograph. (*He crosses to the desk, where there is a large, ornamental ashtray and begins unhurriedly and methodically to clean his pipe.*) It's been circulated to all divisions. Everybody's on the lookout for the girl and the red car.

HOWARD   And what's it got to do with us?

DAVIES   I'm just coming to that. (*Takes out penknife to loosen dottle.*) We believe Julie was alive and in this neighbourhood within a quarter of an hour of your wife's altercation with the street lamp. Just before that occurred, it small red car was parked over the way – empty.

HOWARD   I shouldn't take my wife's word for that – she isn't certain of what she saw.

DAVIES   No, but Mrs Purdie is. She cycled past here on her way to the garage at two minutes to ten exactly. Mind you, the car didn't hang about long – at ten minutes past ten, Will Purdie left his workshop to take a phone call in the sales kiosk outside – from your missus, as a matter of fact – and he was standing there talking when this car went past like a streak of lightning – (*Knocks pipe on ashtray.*) – heading south.

HOWARD   The same car?

DAVIES   He's almost certain of it.

HOWARD   Was anyone with him at the time? His wife, for
            instance?

DAVIES   (*smiles*) No, she was still in the workshop.

            (HOWARD *shrugs and turns his back, as though
            this fact negates the evidence.*)

DAVIES   But then we've got Miss Cunningham to contend
            with.

HOWARD   (*stops*) What's she been saying?

DAVIES   She saw the car about the time the crash occurred.

HOWARD   (*turns*) My – wife's – crash?

DAVIES   Yes, of course. (*He begins to scrape the inside of
            the pipe's bowl with his penknife.*) Miss
            Cunningham claims it didn't stay long after that –
            a fact supported by your good wife, who says that
            after telephoning the police she went outside
            again and found the red car had gone. Whoever
            was in it tore off in a hurry to avoid being dragged
            in as a witness – (*He knocks carbon into the
            ashtray.*) – according to Mrs Holt.

HOWARD   Have you any reason to doubt her word?

DAVIES   Look at all that muck. I'll have to get a filter for
            this thing.

HOWARD   Look here, Inspector –

DAVIES   (*holds it up*) Birthday present from my wife. I've
            been trying to break it in for three months. It still
            tastes like a sewer.

            (HOWARD *breaks off to go and refill his glass.*
            DAVIES *smiles.*)

DAVIES   I'll have a whisky then, if you insist.

HOWARD   Sorry, I thought it wasn't usual for a policeman to drink on duty.

DAVIES   I'm not a usual policeman. (*He blows into his pipe. It is still clogged.*)

HOWARD   (*pours*) Soda?   *You're gone into a (?) detail here*

DAVIES   No thanks, I'm a perfectionist. (*Sits.*)

HOWARD   (*brings drinks*) You were saying?

DAVIES   Ta. (*Puts it by him.*) Where did I get to?

HOWARD   My wife's statement.

DAVIES   Oh, yes. Now let's examine that, in relation to Will Purdie's. Mrs Holt says the car left here at two minutes past ten. Mr Purdie says it shot past his garage not a second before ten past, Difference in time, eight minutes – distance covered, half a mile, conclusion – it wasn't going very fast. Or someone isn't telling us the truth.

HOWARD   Will could have made a mistake, his watch might have been wrong.

DAVIES   Possible, but unlikely – he's the local referee. In any event, we can easily check by asking your wife what time she telephoned him. If she says it was ten past ten, Will must be right. But what we've got to work out then is what this car was doing between the time she says it left and the time Will saw it pass the garage. That might take a bit of explaining. (*Blows into pipe again.*) Damn this thing, it's blocked up! (*He pulls the stem away and digs at it.*)

DAVIES   Here's another thing – when Mrs Purdie saw the car it was empty. I asked her how she knew and she said it was an open two-seater with the hood down. The light was shining directly on it from the street lamp. Two minutes later, your wife went slap-bang into that because the light was out.

HOWARD   That's not beyond the bounds of coincidence.

DAVIES   I'm ready to accept the light gave out in those two
         minutes – but what I find too coincidental is that
         all this followed closely on the last recorded
         appearance of Miss Julie Grant. (*He fits the pipe
         together again.*) Which brings us back to where
         we started.

HOWARD   I thought you said the girl drove back again past
         Purdie's Garage ten minutes later?

DAVIES   No. I said the car went by, I didn't say who was
         driving it. By that time the hood was up.

HOWARD   Bad luck.

DAVIES   It might have been luck; on the other hand, it
         might have been deliberate. (*Pause.*) Will Purdie
         says it was a man. (HOWARD *meets his gaze.*)

HOWARD   (*steadily*) You haven't finished your drink,
         Inspector.

DAVIES   I haven't started it yet. (*Picks it up.*) Mind you,
         we don't know who this fellow was, he was going
         too fast for that. It might have been anybody . . .
         even you.

HOWARD   What the devil are you suggesting?

DAVIES   I'm suggesting nothing; I'm telling you – we don't
         know. Now you tell me Mr Holt, what were you
         doing at ten o'clock that night?

HOWARD   That's no concern of yours.

DAVIES   You were out though, weren't you?

HOWARD   Does that make me a suspect?

DAVIES   Just for argument's sake, can you prove you
         weren't driving that car?

HOWARD   Just for argument's sake, can you prove I *was*?

         (*They hold each other's eyes for a split second.*)

~~DAVIES~~   ~~Good health.~~ (*He drinks.*)

HOWARD   Let's be fair about this. It's an intriguing story –
         almost good enough for a book! But in everything
         you've said there's not one fact, not one single,
         solitary fact to suggest foul play.

DAVIES   Who said anything about foul play? There's a lot
         of donkey work ahead before we get as definite as
         that! You see, in cases of this kind – if death is
         suspected –

HOWARD   So you're working on those lines?

DAVIES   (*continues stolidly*) If death is suspected our first
         job is to establish identity. Then we start to ask a
         lot of questions. After that, it's a simple process
         of elimination – all there, in the book.

HOWARD   And somewhere in that book I'm sure there's a
         paragraph devoted to something you've omitted
         to mention. Something without which you've no
         case. The body. Have you got it?

DAVIES   No.

HOWARD   (*confidently*) Find the body, find the suspect, find
         the proof. Isn't that what the book says?

DAVIES   Roughly.

HOWARD   And all you've got to go on is a photograph. It's
         not much.

DAVIES   (*rises*) It's a start. (*He goes to replace his glass.*)

HOWARD   Inspector, do you mind if I ask you a question –
         for a change?

DAVIES   With pleasure, Mr Holt.

HOWARD   Why have you let me in on all this?

DAVIES   (*pleasantly*) I always enjoy your conversation.

HOWARD   I find that hard to believe, since you do all the
              talking.

DAVIES   Let's say it helps me sort out all the facts.

HOWARD   You did that before you came.

DAVIES   Maybe I thought you'd be interested from a
              professional point of view.

HOWARD   Let's agree on one thing: I make my living out of
              fiction – not murder.

DAVIES   That's another word that hasn't been mentioned
              . . . up to now.

HOWARD   (*sits coolly*) Now give me the *real* reason.

              (DAVIES *moves slightly above him and speaks with
              quiet authority.*)

DAVIES   It started with a feeling, Mr Holt. That's how most
              investigations start, with a feeling that everything
              isn't quite as it should be. In this case someone
              told a deliberate lie about a pair of headlights. A
              lie for no apparent reason's always suspicious: it
              sets you thinking. You notice the way a woman
              loses a set of car keys, and when her husband
              produces some and tells you they belong to him,
              you wonder why they should be on a leather tag
              that matches her handbag and the folder that
              contains her driving licence. You ask yourself,
              what's he doing with her keys, when she's already
              told you that he hardly ever drives the car? And
              when she tells another lie – and another – you
              begin to look for motivation.

HOWARD   Minor mistakes, confusion, slips of the tongue –
                these things aren't evidence.

DAVIES   Signposts, Mr Holt – pointing for the most part in
                the wrong direction, but at least they lead you
                somewhere.

                (*Unnoticed by both,* KAREN *comes softly out of the
                bedroom, in her dressing-gown. She looks pale
                and haggard.*)

DAVIES   You take note of little things you might otherwise
                have missed – half-truths and evasions – the look
                on a man's face when he sees a photograph –
                what happens to a woman's nerves, under stress.
                And when these two get jumpy and bad-tempered
                – insulting, even – it begins to dawn on you that
                there's something they're trying to hide.
                Something big. You don't know what it is, but of
                this you're certain – they're covering up the truth.
                So that's what you set out to find.

KAREN   (*curtly*) How far have you got?

                (*The men turn.* HOWARD *jumps up.*)

HOWARD   Karen you shouldn't be up.

KAREN   I'm all right. (*To* DAVIES.) Why don't you answer?

HOWARD   I refuse to let you speak to my wife in this
                condition.

DAVIES   (*quietly*) Your husband's right, Mrs Holt. (KAREN
                wrenches away from HOWARD *and comes for him.*)

KAREN   What do you want with us – why can't you leave
                us alone?

DAVIES   I wish I could, I'm only doing the job I'm paid for.

KAREN   (*sways*) I'm sorry. Forgive me. I – I haven't been
                well. (*She sits.*)

DAVIES   I'll come back in a day or two.

KAREN   No! I can't stand much more of this. What is it this time?

DAVIES   (*produces photograph*) With your permission, sir? (HOWARD *is powerless.*)

DAVIES   I was wondering, Mrs Holt, if you could possibly identify this young woman? (*He holds it before her.*)

HOWARD   Karen, you don't have to –

DAVIES   (*sharply*) Please. Let her speak. (*Long pause.*)

KAREN   I've never seen her before in my life. (HOWARD *looks in triumph at* DAVIES.)

DAVIES   I see. (*Puts it away.*)

KAREN   Now will you please go,

DAVIES   One other question, if you don't mind. Can you remember what time you telephoned Purdie's Garage on Friday, September the fourth? (KAREN *looks up at her husband. His face is a mask.*)

KAREN   (*turns*) It was ten minutes past ten.

DAVIES   You're sure?

KAREN   I checked the time.

DAVIES   Thank you. (*Looks at* HOWARD.) That's all I want to know. (*He makes for the door.*)

HOWARD   Inspector, if you honestly believe this girl is dead . . .

            (KAREN *swings round.*)

DAVIES   She's missing, Mr Holt – let's leave it at that, shall we? Perhaps the search will tell us a bit more.

KAREN   (*whispers*) Search?

DAVIES   We've been covering this area pretty thoroughly
            for the past few days. There's still a few more
            acres left – (*To* HOWARD.) – to the south . . . then I
            think we can call it a day. (*To door.*)

HOWARD   (*harshly*) That was one thing you left out.

DAVIES   (*turns*) Come sir, you don't expect me to give
            away all my little secrets, do you? "Find the body,
            find the suspect, find the proof" – those were
            your very words. Good advice, that – I'd call it
            almost professional. Good afternoon. (*He touches
            his hat to them and departs. Long pause.*)

KAREN   So he knows.

HOWARD   He knows nothing.

KAREN   That picture –

HOWARD   Some drunken old fool of a father reported her
            missing, that's all they know.

KAREN   And if they find her?

HOWARD   They won't.

KAREN   How can you be so sure?

HOWARD   She's miles away from here, deep down at the
            bottom of a ~~swamp~~ they couldn't drag, even if
            they knew which one it was. I'd stake my life on it.

KAREN   We may have to – both of us. (*She rises to the
            window.*)

KAREN   Somewhere – out there now – men are searching.

HOWARD   She's safe enough.

KAREN   If it hadn't been for me, she'd be alive today. Last night I had that dream again: it's coming more and more often. You're sitting in a car, your fingers frozen to the wheel. It's going faster-faster-faster.

HOWARD   Stop it, Karen.

KAREN   I wish to heaven I could but I can't shut out the memory of it – don't you think I've tried, all these weeks? That night's burned its way into my brain and nothing's ever going to rid me of it. I can't stand any more, I've got to tell the police!

(*She plunges for the phone. He blocks her way.*)

HOWARD   Are you out of your mind?

KAREN   It's better than the way we're living now – I'm going to finish it, finish it once and for all.

HOWARD   What are you going to tell them?

KAREN   Everything! How she died, and what we did, about the money we've been sending and the letters –

HOWARD   No, Karen!

KAREN   Can't you see, it's the only way I can stay sane?

(*They face each other across the phone.*)

HOWARD   What is it you want, to be shut up, locked away for the rest of your life? That's the least they'll do.

KAREN   It was an accident, they'll believe me, they've *got* to believe me (*She lifts the phone.*)

HOWARD   They'll believe you all right – but use the right words!

(*His hand comes down on the hook and severs the connection.*)

HOWARD   Tell them how you murdered Julie Grant!

(*Her head jerks back.*)

HOWARD   Does that word frighten you? Don't let it. That's the word they'll put on the indictment, the word they'll splash across the pages at your trial, the word you've got to live with from now on . . . *murder.*

(*He releases the hook.*)

HOWARD   Go ahead and tell 'em.

(*Slowly, without taking her eyes from his face,* KAREN *replaces the phone.*)

KAREN   Howard, you don't – you can't believe that I –

HOWARD   It's not what I believe, it's what they believe that counts. You heard what Davies said – "something big". He's stopped looking for a missing girl, he's started looking for a murderer.

KAREN   It wasn't murder! I knew nothing about the girl – who she was or where she came from! Would I have telephoned the police?

HOWARD   Why did you? That's what they'll want to know. Why did you telephone the police – *and not a* ~~doctor?~~ *ambulance* ?

KAREN   I was in a panic – she was lying still.

HOWARD   You knew she was dead because you killed her in cold blood.

KAREN   (*backs*) That isn't true – you know it isn't true!

HOWARD   Look at the facts, see it their way. The girl and I were lovers. You arrived ten minutes after she did – ten minutes! They'll say you followed her from London. You sat outside in the car waiting,

wondering what to do. You knew she was here,
you could see her in my arms –

KAREN   (*in agony*) Don't, Howard –

HOWARD   Then this door flew open. You heard footsteps on
the drive. You pressed the starter, threw her into
gear and moved in for the kill.

KAREN   I tried to stop it! I caught her for a moment in the
lights and swung the wheel hard over, but it was
too late – she'd gone down like a stone. Somehow
I got out of the car. She was lying still. Then – I
ran!

HOWARD   You expect Davies to believe that?

KAREN   It's the truth. I swear it was an accident.

HOWARD   Do you, Karen? (*Grabs her wrists.*) What if I
swear it was murder?

KAREN   (*stares wildly*) What are you saying?

HOWARD   Six weeks ago you killed a girl and I concealed the
body. Do you know what that means? Jail for us
both, if the truth comes out. (*Pushes her away.*)
I'm the only material witness – call in the police
and I'll swear you did it deliberately. Tell Davies
the truth and I'll put you in the dock on a charge
of murder. I mean it. Karen – every word. (*She still
stares, soundlessly.*)

KAREN   (*finally*) You – could – do – that? (*He unhooks the
receiver and offers it to her.*)

HOWARD   Try me. (KAREN *cracks.*)

KAREN   God help me! (*She collapses in a chair.*)

HOWARD   Now perhaps, you'll see sense and do it my way.
Davies can go on with the inquiry – without a
body he's working in the dark. They'll never break

our story and *they'll never find her.* (*He selects a cigarette.*)

HOWARD There's only one real danger – the man who wrote those letters. I'll find a way to deal with him, once he agrees to come out in the open. (*He lights his cigarette.*)

HOWARD Something quick – and certain. A powerful car, perhaps – (*Glances at her.*) – on a lonely road – at night. (*The telephone rings.*)

HOWARD Talk of the devil. (*Checks watch.*) He's early. (*It still rings.*)

HOWARD Answer it. (KAREN *drags herself to her feet and does so.*)

KAREN Hello? Yes. (*Waits.*) Thank you, I – (*She hangs up abruptly and stares at the receiver.*)

KAREN You were wrong, Howard. That was the police. (*Faces him.*) They've found her. (HOWARD *whirls to face her.* KAREN *falls in a dead faint.*)

(*Blackout.*)

ACT THREE

Scene One

The same. Shortly afterwards.

KAREN *lies full-length on the settee. A drink is near her,*
ready-poured for her awakening. HOWARD *is at the desk,*
packing papers into a briefcase. His raincoat is at hand.
KAREN *stirs.*

KAREN   (*dazed*) What . . . what's happening?

            (*She tries to sit up. He brings her the drink.*)

HOWARD   Take it easy. Everything's under control.

KAREN   How long have I been –

HOWARD   Here.

KAREN   Your coat . . . and that bag. Where are you –
            (*Struggles up.*) – what are you going to do?

HOWARD   Isn't it obvious?

KAREN   (*drink down*) You're leaving?

HOWARD   I'm leaving. (*Examines his passport and drops it*
            into bag.) There, I think that's the lot.

KAREN   But you can't – only a few minutes ago you said

HOWARD   I know what I said. But circumstances alter cases,
            especially murder cases.

KAREN   You're walking out? You expect me to face all this
            alone?

HOWARD   I'm afraid so.

KAREN   You could have gone while I was still
            unconscious. Why didn't you?

HOWARD   I wanted some information first. That was Davies
          on the telephone, wasn't it?

KAREN   Yes.

HOWARD   What exactly did he say?

KAREN   Does that matter – now?

HOWARD   It does to me.

KAREN   He said, "I thought you ought to know we've
          found what we were looking for."

HOWARD   Nothing else?

KAREN   I hung up.

HOWARD   That was twenty minutes ago. I've been expecting
          them ever since. They haven't come.

KAREN   They will.

HOWARD   I wonder. They've got a body and we're under
          suspicion – yet they haven't come. Tell me
          something, Karen – if you were out to catch a rat,
          would you show him the trap first and let him see
          how it worked? It doesn't make sense.

KAREN   Nothing does, any more.

HOWARD   But if you weren't quite sure – if you had him
          cornered and were waiting for him to jump – if you
          were the inspector and you had a corpse, a
          suspect and *no proof* . . . isn't it likely you'd
          throw out a scrap of information to see what effect
          it had on a guilty conscience?

KAREN   If that's it, aren't you doing exactly what he wants
          by running away?

HOWARD   I don't think so, as long as one of us stays. I'm
          going to London . . . there's nothing very guilty
          about that, I often go.

KAREN   And what do you expect me to say to him?

HOWARD   You can say anything you like . . . after I've gone.

KAREN   Because London isn't the end of the line, is it, Howard?

HOWARD   Not by a long chalk. I'll only be there long enough to catch a plane. I booked my seat on the phone while you were asleep.

             (KAREN *smiles bitterly and rises.*)

KAREN   Is she very beautiful?

HOWARD   Who?

KAREN   The girl called Terry.

             (*He looks at her in surprise.*)

KAREN   I was listening in there when she phoned.

HOWARD   Clever of you – and I thought we'd been cut off. Still, I'm glad you know. It saves further explanations.

KAREN   I should have realised Julie wasn't the only one.

HOWARD   She wasn't the first – and I don't suppose she'll be the last.

KAREN   And you honestly think you'll get away?

HOWARD   With luck – and your cooperation.

KAREN   What makes you think I'd lift a finger to help you?

HOWARD   I don't. The word I used was "cooperation". By helping me you help yourself. I'm offering you your freedom.

KAREN   I'm sorry, Howard, this is one time I can't follow
          your fantasies. What I'm up against is real . . . it's
          final.

HOWARD   Not if you do as I say. All that's need and a little
          nerve. You've got plenty of both.

          (*He picks up a letter at the desk, takes a sheet of
          paper from it and tosses the envelope back on the
          desk.*)

          Exhibit One – the latest *Billet-doux* from our
          blackmailing friend. Read it.

          (*He takes it to her.*)

KAREN   Why? It's just like all the others.

HOWARD   Exactly. It blames me, not you. They all do. Ask
          yourself what Miss Cunningham saw that night –
          me, not you. Will Purdie watched a car tear past
          his garage – he can't say who was driving it but
          he knows it was a man. Can't you see what I'm
          getting at?

          (*She stares at him dully.*)

HOWARD   When the police came I was out. I haven't got
          an alibi. As far as anyone knows, I'm the
          guilty party. Everything fits – it only needs
          someone to put the pieces together. Davies might
          get round to it in time but you can save him the
          trouble. Tell him you lied to shield me. Miss
          Cunningham will back you up, Will Purdie, too – I
          shan't be here to defend myself. You can blame me
          for everything and I'll let you do it – for the
          chance to make a getaway and the money you've
          got in the safe.

KAREN   Aren't you forgetting? The money's there for a
          purpose.

HOWARD   The blackmailer?

KAREN   He'd never be able to find you but he'd still have
           me. The letters would go on.

HOWARD   I've told you, every single one of them blames *me*.

KAREN   (*at desk*) They came from London, didn't they?

HOWARD   As far as we know.

KAREN   (*picks up envelope*) And this arrived this
           morning?

HOWARD   First post.

KAREN   Why hasn't it got a postmark?

HOWARD   They get missed sometimes, I've known it happen.

KAREN   (*turns it over*) It wasn't even sealed.

HOWARD   (*shrugs*) Careless of me, but then – I was
           interrupted.

KAREN   (*unable to believe her senses*) You – wrote – this?

HOWARD   I wrote them all.

           (*She crumples it slowly in her hand and lets it
           fall to the carpet.*)

KAREN   Week after week . . . the agony of it . . . you
           swine!

HOWARD   Agreed. But rather clever, don't you think?

           (*Her fingers close on a paper-knife.*)

KAREN   You – !

           (*She goes for him wildly, raising it high in the
           air. He clamps her wrist in a grip of steel.*)

HOWARD   Let go – let go!

(*He turns her up-stage and forces her hand down.
The weapon leaves her grasp. He pushes her
roughly aside and stoops to retrieve it.*)

KAREN   What kind of man are you?

HOWARD   A kind you'd never understand. Open the safe.

KAREN   To think I loved you!

HOWARD   You were ready enough to pay the blackmailer.
             Nothing's changed – except now you know who
             you're paying and what you're paying for.

KAREN   I thought nothing could kill that love. God knows I
             had reason to hate you before today, but through
             right and wrong I went on loving you. Now you've
             destroyed that love – destroyed *me*!

HOWARD   The money, Karen.

             (*She stares at him in sheer contempt. Then she
             shakes her head.*)

KAREN   I've finished, Howard.

             (*He moves towards her, raising the knife slightly.*)

HOWARD   I could make you . . .

             (*She faces it – and him.*)

KAREN   Go ahead, Do you think there's anything you can
             do that could hurt me more than you have already?
             Well, what are you waiting for? Why don't you kill
             me, too?

             (*He starts slightly and lowers the knife.*)

             That's the real truth, isn't it? Out there on the
             road that night – *you finished what I started.*
             That's why you're certain it'll be a murder charge,
             that's what you've been afraid of all along – that's
             why you're running now.

(*He stares at her a moment.*)

HOWARD   Damn you.

           (*He tosses the knife from him and, picking up his
           things, makes for the door.*)

KAREN   (*sharply*) Wait!

           (*He halts.*)

KAREN   All right. Howard, you can have the money – all of
           it – on one condition.

HOWARD   Well?

KAREN   First, tell me – this girl Terry. She knows
           something. She helped you with the letters –
           someone must have.

HOWARD   She posted them from London.

KAREN   And the phone calls?

HOWARD   Prearranged. I took them all.

KAREN   Except today.

HOWARD   That turned out to be Davies.

KAREN   And the first one of all. A man rang up – ~~the maid~~ Stella
           answered.

HOWARD   A little refinement of my own to add conviction. I
           went out specially that morning to do it.

KAREN   So there were no witnesses. *No one saw.*

HOWARD   You have my word.

KAREN   Your word isn't good enough any more, unless it's
           down in writing.

HOWARD   Is that the condition?

KAREN   The money – and the letters – in exchange for a signed confession, written as I dictate it. Those are my terms, Howard – my only terms.

HOWARD   And if they're not acceptable?

KAREN   The minute you leave I get on to the Inspector. You'll never reach London. Anything you do to try and stop me will only make it worse for you. (*Pause.*) Well?

HOWARD   I always said you were intelligent.

(*He drops his case and sits at the desk, his back to her.*)

HOWARD   What shall I put?

KAREN   "To whom it may concern . . . " That's customary, I believe.

(*He reaches for a pen and writes.*)

KAREN   "I killed Julie Grant."

(*He looks at her once, then scribbles rapidly. KAREN crosses to a picture on the wall, which she swings back on hinges to reveal a small, modern wall safe. Her back is towards us as she works the combination and swings back the door. She reaches inside for something. As she returns to HOWARD through what follows, one hand is in her dressing-gown pocket and the other holds six or seven letters, all in identical envelopes.*)

KAREN   (*continues*) "My wife has lied to shield me, but realising the truth is bound to come out – I write this to absolve her from all blame."

(*She tosses the letters on the desk.*)

HOWARD   And the money?

KAREN   When you've finished.

            (*He carries on, then leans back to read what he
            has written. She faces him across the desk, both
            hands in her pockets.*)

HOWARD   Anything else?

KAREN   (*bitterly*) You can say, "Forgive me, Karen."

            (*He bends forward to do this and she moves above
            him, facing out front.*)

KAREN   Now sign it.

            (*As he does so she takes her hand from her pocket
            – it holds a small revolver. She puts it to his right
            temple and pulls the trigger. A shot rings out.
            HOWARD is flung forward and sideways by the
            impact, then he sprawls across the downstage
            corner of his desk, dead. KAREN recoils for a
            moment, then quickly carries out the rest of her
            plan. She pockets the blackmail letters, then
            takes out a handkerchief to wipe the gun clean of
            her fingerprints before pressing the butt carefully
            between his lifeless fingers. Finally, she reaches
            for HOWARD's confession and scans quickly
            through it before folding the sheet in two and
            propping it against her picture. Then she picks
            up the telephone.*)

KAREN   Give me the police.

            (*Blackout.*)

*Author's Note: For maximum effect, it is important that we
should not guess KAREN's intentions before she actually
shoots HOWARD. And in the interests of safety, coupled with
conviction, the gun shot itself should be done by stage
management, off R. A visual cue may be taken by means of the
direct sightline through the window to the desk.*

Scene Two

The same. The next morning.

INSPECTOR DAVIES *is going through letters and documents at the desk, and packing selected items in a black, official-looking case.* KAREN *sits quietly, hands clasped in the centre of the room. She wears an appropriately dark suit or dress.*

DAVIES   I'll take these with me if you've no objection?

KAREN   What?

DAVIES   (*holds papers out*) I said I'll take –

KAREN   Yes, please do. I don't mind.

DAVIES   You'll get the usual report.

          (*No answer. He stows them away and comes nearer to her.*)

          Mrs Holt, I'm more sorry than I can say about all this. If you feel you'd rather not go on –

KAREN   I must. I must know everything.

DAVIES   It's up to you.

KAREN   Inspector, first I'd like to thank you for not making me talk last night.

DAVIES   We wouldn't have go much sense out of you, would we, not after a shock like that?

KAREN   It was most considerate. You've gone out of your way to make things easier

DAVIES   All part of the job.

KAREN   (*rises*) Let's carry on, shall we? I can't rest until you know it all.

DAVIES   Whatever you say. Now then . . . we've got the
               general picture of your husband's association
               with this girl and the events leading up to the
               night of September fourth. (*Sits.*) I think you'd
               better tell me the rest of it in your own words.

KAREN   Shouldn't there be someone here to take down a
               statement?

DAVIES   No, that'll come later. All I want for now is to get
               things straight in my own mind.

KAREN   Very well. (*Pause.*) I drove up here about ten
               o'clock that night, left the car outside and walked
               up the drive. I let myself in with my own key. I
               remember the radio playing. The girl was lying
               there . . . dead. I was horrified. I searched the
               place for Howard but he was nowhere to be found.
               Then I telephoned the police. Howard came in as I
               started talking, guessed the situation and
               snatched the phone out of my hand. Then he told
               me what he'd done. He'd killed the girl because
               he'd tired of her but she wouldn't leave him alone
               – she was pestering him, threatening to contact me
               and make trouble. So he invited her for the
               weekend and when she arrived he offered to put
               her car away. She went out with him to open the
               garage doors – (*Nods towards kitchen.*) – round
               this side of the house, as you know. As she was
               crossing back, he – ran her down. (*Looks at him.*)
               You knew that was how she died?

DAVIES   We had an idea but we couldn't be absolutely
               sure. I wonder why he brought the body indoors?

KAREN   To keep her hidden, I suppose, while he went back
               to cover his tracks. When he came in and found
               me here he begged me not to give him away. I tried
               to reason with him – told him the police were
               coming – but at that he grew hysterical and
               threatened to kill himself if I didn't help him. I had

to do as he said. Then he invented the accident to
my car and went off to make the arrangements.

DAVIES   And the girl?

KAREN   He said he'd take her far away, somewhere she'd
never be found. That's why I was alone when you
came along and so unnerved I made all those
foolish mistakes.

DAVIES   The headlights, you mean? (*She nods.*)

DAVIES   And of course your husband had the car keys.

KAREN   You arrived before he could get them back to me.
The whole thing was insane, we should have
known it couldn't work; but then, we never
anticipated having you to deal with. Afterwards,
Howard said we must stay on to allay suspicion.
We hired a maid and tried to live a normal life.
That was the beginning of a long nightmare for
me. Every time you came I grew more and more
convinced you knew something. It began to tell on
my nerves. Yesterday you told us the girl had
been reported missing. After you'd gone I pleaded
with him to own up but he only laughed at me. He
said you'd never find the body – he seemed so
sure of that.

DAVIES   They always are.

KAREN   Then you telephoned to say you'd found her and
we knew it was all over. I told him I was going to
the police station and begged him to come to with
me. He wouldn't listen. I started out alone, but
half way to the village I lost my nerve and ran
back to be with him. When I came in – (*Softly.*) –
you know what I found.

(*She pauses.* DAVIES *leans forward.*)

DAVIES   Could you tell me about the gun, Mrs Holt? It's
registered in your name.

KAREN   Yes, it used to belong to my father. When he died,
             Howard took charge of it, along with everything
             else here. It was always kept in the safe. I never
             dreamed that one day he'd – he'd . . .

             (*She chokes.* DAVIES *rises.*)

DAVIES   Thank you. I think that'll be all, for now. Can I get
             you something to drink?

KAREN   No, thank you, nothing.

DAVIES   (*starts L*) Perhaps I'd better call the girl.

KAREN   She isn't here. I sent her away last night after
             you'd questioned her.

DAVIES   (*surprised*) You spent the night alone here?

KAREN   That's how I wanted it, Inspector. I'll be all right –
             it's just reaction. That – and the relief at being
             able to unburden myself. Now I'll get my coat and
             come with you.

DAVIES   (*gently*) I don't think that'll be necessary, Mrs
             Holt. Not for awhile, at any rate.

             (*She glances at him.*)

DAVIES   Surprised? I'm much obliged to you for all you've
             told me, it answers quite a lot. But I can't take you
             into custody – without further confirmation.

KAREN   But you have Miss Cunningham's evidence, and
             Will Purdie's. You know Howard never had an alibi
             for that night –

DAVIES   (*back at desk, closing case*) That's all true, but it
             isn't quite enough.

KAREN   But now you've got his signed confession and my
             statement to back it up –

DAVIES   We've got all the evidence we want – now all we
            need is *proof.*

            (*He snaps the lock on his case. His back is to
            her.*)

DAVIES   Incidentally, did Mr Holt ever tell you where he'd
            put the body?

KAREN   No. He said only he must know.

DAVIES   Never mind – we'll find it, sooner or later. (KAREN
            is stunned.)

KAREN   You mean you – haven't found her?

DAVIES   (*turns*) No. But we will.

KAREN   If this is some kind of joke, Inspector, it's in the
            worst possible taste –

DAVIES   I never joke, Mrs Holt – about murder.

KAREN   But you telephoned! You said, "We've found what
            we were looking for."

DAVIES   You wouldn't let me finish, would you? You cut
            me off. I was talking about the car.

            (KAREN *gasps.*)

DAVIES   It was found abandoned in a London car park,
            minus registration plates. That's why it's taken so
            long to trace.

KAREN   Don't you realise what this means? If Howard had
            known that, I –

            (*She stops, abruptly.*)

DAVIES   Yes, Mrs Holt?

KAREN   You did it on purpose. Howard was right, you set
            a trap to find out what we'd do.

DAVIES   Believe that if you wish.

KAREN   So this is how the police work, through lies and
                trickery!

DAVIES   No – but we reserve the right. (*Quiet and
                compelling.*) I spend my life dealing with people
                who specialise in evil, who live by lies and
                trickery. What do you expect me to do – treat them
                with respect?

KAREN   Try to think of them at least as human beings –

DAVIES   A being without a conscience isn't human. (*To
                door.*) By the way, you won't try and leave the
                district, will you?

KAREN   Are you asking me or telling me?

DAVIES   Whichever you think appropriate.

KAREN   I thought of going to a hotel.

DAVIES   There's nothing to stop you, as long as it's
                somewhere local – but don't forget to let us have
                the telephone number.

KAREN   (*boldly*) *Why*, Inspector?

DAVIES   You'll be wanted at the inquest.

                (*He goes. As the door closes she stares after him,
                then walks to the desk. She gazes at her
                husband's picture. Over her shoulder, across the
                room, the door-knob clicks softly as someone
                turns it on the other side.* KAREN *turns slowly and
                watches it, not knowing quite what to expect. The
                door opens and a girl walks into the room. It is*
                JULIE. KAREN *gasps and falls back, leaning on the
                desk.*)

JULIE   Morning, Mrs Holt.

KAREN   Who are you?

JULIE   Julie Grant. (*Pause.*) Sorry for sneaking in the
         back, I didn't want to be seen. I thought it was
         better that way, for both of us.

KAREN   It isn't true – it can't be – Julie Grant's dead!

JULIE   You only thought she was.

KAREN   (*sits*) All these weeks – where've you been
         hiding?

JULIE   London, under another name.

KAREN   That night – out there – you lay so still.

JULIE   I passed out when the car hit me.

KAREN   And you weren't hurt – at all?

JULIE   Cut and bruised. My shoulder was pretty bad. But
         you must have swerved at the last minute, it was
         only the wing that caught me. When I came to,
         Howard was driving me away. He put me on a train
         with orders to keep my mouth shut. I got to
         London and booked into a cheap hotel under
         another name – Terry Matthews.

KAREN   Terry! It was you who sent the letters.

JULIE   I didn't know what was in them – Howard wrote
         them.

KAREN   I know.

JULIE   A few days later he brought the car down, dumped
         it somewhere and came round to see me. He said
         he'd found a way of getting all the cash we
         needed so we could go away together. All I had to
         do was lie low and post the letter week by week. I
         never guessed what he was really up to – I
         thought I was being kept under cover for quite a
         different reason. Then two days ago I went out to

post one of the letters and something stopped me.
I took it into an ABC and read it over a cup of
coffee. I didn't post it – instead I tore it up.

KAREN   That's why he wrote the duplicate in a hurry.

JULIE   Duplicate?

KAREN   Never mind – go on.

JULIE   I couldn't sleep that night for worrying – I never
          asked to be mixed up in blackmail! Yesterday I
          rang him on this phone and said if he didn't tell
          you the truth and clear me I'd come here and do it
          for him. He said he'd come and see me at the
          weekend. This morning I opened the paper and
          read what he'd done.

          (*She tosses a morning paper on the desk.*)

KAREN   (*steadily*) Why are you here?

JULIE   (*hesitates*) He – told you everything, I suppose?

KAREN   Enough.

JULIE   And you've passed it on to the police?

KAREN   Not all.

JULIE   Then they still don't know I'm alive? – that's what
          I came to find out.

          (*No answer.*)

          You don't have to answer. I saw your face as I
          walked in – you looked as though you'd seen a
          ghost.

KAREN   My husband taught you a lot, didn't he?

JULIE   I taught myself! (*Bitterly.*) I'm learning all the
          time.

KAREN   Take it from me, Julie, you're only a beginner.

JULIE   You've got to give me a chance, Mrs Holt –

KAREN   Don't worry. You're safe enough for the moment.

JULIE   And you won't tell them?

KAREN   I don't know yet.

JULIE   (*desperately*) You've got to believe me! Howard
            forced me into it – used me just as he used you
            and everybody – but none of it was my fault!

KAREN   (*rounds on her*) How dare you come here crawling
            for sympathy? You knew all about it, you were in
            it from the start. You posted all the letters, you
            helped him with the phone calls . . . and when you
            telephoned yesterday it wasn't because you'd
            grown a halo overnight – oh no, it was a lot
            simpler than that. You were scared. He'd never let
            you have a penny and you couldn't wait for your
            share, You threatened to betray him, yes – but
            only if he broke his promise to you.

JULIE   Is that what he told you?

KAREN   It's what I heard for myself – I was listening on
            the extension when you phoned. You suddenly
            woke up to something, didn't you, Julie? That
            he'd keep all the profits for himself and then walk
            out on both of us. And you were dead right.

JULIE   You know it all, don't you? (*Defiantly.*) All right
            I'm as much to blame as he was, I did everything
            he said because I had to!

KAREN   Why, for what reason?

JULIE   The best reason I know! (*Simply.*) I'm going to
            have his child.

            (*This comes as a blow between the eyes for*
            KAREN.)

JULIE   Now do you understand? How do you think I felt
             when I read that paper? You see, I loved him –
             too.

             (*Long pause.*)

KAREN   You're sure nobody followed you here?

JULIE   Positive.

KAREN   And you'll never come again?

JULIE   I'm not that crazy. If you keep quiet about me, this
             is the last time you'll see me.

KAREN   All right.

             (JULIE *rises.*)

KAREN   Wait.

             (*She goes to the safe and takes out a bulky bank
             envelope.*)

KAREN   Here's some money. Enough to keep both of you,
             for quite a time.

             (*She tosses it in a chair near* JULIE.)

JULIE   I didn't come here for charity –

KAREN   Take it. But remember, Grant's dead – she stays
             dead.

             (JULIE *looks at the money. Finally she picks it up,
             then looks at* KAREN.)

JULIE   (*softly*) He didn't deserve you.

KAREN   You didn't ask for charity, I don't ask for pity.
             Now get out.

             (*Door buzzer.*)

KAREN   Quickly – the way you came!

             (*She urges* JULIE *off L.*)

KAREN   And for God's sake be careful! (JULIE *slips out
             through the kitchen. The buzzer goes again.*
             KAREN *closes the door L and hurries back to the
             safe to lock it and swing the picture back into
             place. She answers the door.* WILL PURDIE *stands
             outside.*)

KAREN   (*relieved*) Will – it's you.

WILL   Sorry to trouble you, mum. Could I use your
             phone?

KAREN   Certainly. Come in.

WILL   (*enters to phone*) 'Ta very much. (*Picks it up.*)
             Double-three please, miss.

KAREN   What's the trouble?

WILL   The breakdown van's broke down.

KAREN   I'm sorry.

WILL   I won't be a minute.

KAREN   There's no hurry.

             (*She goes off into the bedroom.*)

WILL   (*into phone*) That you, Gert? Lizzie's gone again.
             Same old distributor. Listen, girl – you know that
             little box of allsorts in the corner? Not the first-aid
             box, ducky, the one down underneath. You'll find
             a spare part in there – hop on the old bike and
             bring it over, will you? I'm at Mrs – *punctured?*
             (*Raises his eyes to heaven.*) What a flaming
             garage! Never mind, I'll come back and do it
             myself.

              (*He hangs up.* KAREN *enters with a coat and a packed weekend case.*)

WILL   Thanks, Mrs Holt. Now let's see – (*Jangles coins in pocket.*) – that'll be –

KAREN   Forget it, Will.

WILL   Very nice of you. (*To door.*) By the way, mum – Gert and me, we're very sorry; about Mr Holt, I mean.

KAREN   Thank you.

WILL   Well, I'd better be off.

              (*He opens the door.* DAVIES *is on the threshold.*)

WILL   Blimey!

DAVIES   Sorry, Will. I had my finger on the bell.

KAREN   Inspector – do come in.

DAVIES   Thank you. (*Crosses* WILL.) I hope I'm not intruding?

WILL   No more than usual. Good bye, mum. (*He leaves.*)

KAREN   Yes, Inspector?

DAVIES   I'm sorry to be such a nuisance. I fancy I left my pipe somewhere about.

              (*He goes to the desk and hunts, lifting the newspaper.*)

DAVIES   Yes, here it is. (*Replaces paper.*) The wife'd never forgive me if I lost this. I keep on trying to!

              (*Sucking at the stem, he glances at the paper . . .* JULIE'S *paper.*)

KAREN   Anything else on your mind, Inspector?

DAVIES	There is one thing, Mrs Holt. You know you said your husband took the body far away?
KAREN	That's what he told me.
DAVIES	He was back here within half an hour, talking to me.
KAREN	He went out again after you'd gone.
DAVIES	Ah. (*Pause.*) Suppose that was just to pull the wool over your eyes because he had to get rid of the car? Suppose he got the girl away the first time – on a train, for instance?
KAREN	That's impossible.
DAVIES	Not altogether. There's a train to London every night about that time.
KAREN	The girl was dead.
DAVIES	We've only got your word for that.
KAREN	And my husband's, in his note.
DAVIES	That, too. But we've combed this area, Mrs Holt, and there isn't a sign of her. (*Whimsically.*) To tell truth, I'm beginning to wonder if she ever died at all.
KAREN	If this is another trick –
DAVIES	Maybe you *believed* she was dead and helped to conceal her disappearance in case it might incriminate you – personally.
KAREN	I've told you I was shielding Howard.
DAVIES	What if it was the other way round? What if he was shielding you?
KAREN	Why? What possible reason could he have?

DAVIES   Only one – if he didn't run her down that night
          but *you did.*

KAREN   You can't be serious –

DAVIES   If you did, and thought you'd killed her, then got
          your husband to help you – that would explain
          everything that happened after I turned up. It
          would further explain why you fell such an easy
          victim to blackmail.

KAREN   Blackmail!

DAVIES   You've made regular withdrawals from the bank
          lately. Heavy withdrawals . . . in cash.

KAREN   I've had some heavy expenses.

DAVIES   Such as?

KAREN   I can't remember details –

DAVIES   Details, Mrs Holt – amounting to more than two
          thousand pounds? Can you deny that letters have
          been coming here, demanding money with
          menaces?

KAREN   That's a lie –

DAVIES   It's the truth! You picked the wrong sort of maid,
          you know. She grew downright inquisitive . . . is
          that why you got rid of her, in case she talked too
          much?

KAREN   I won't have people prying into my personal
          affairs.

DAVIES   I'm afraid that's something you'll have to get used
          to, from now on.

KAREN   All right! I admit the letters came and I paid, each
          time. Where does that get you, Inspector? They
          were unsigned – nobody knows who wrote them.

DAVIES   You're wrong, Mrs Holt. I know.

              (*He takes from his wallet a folded sheet of
              coloured blotting paper.*)

DAVIES   This came from the blotter on your desk. I took it
              last night, while you were in the bedroom with the
              doctor. It's got the impression of a letter on it, or
              part of one. It doesn't tell us everything but
              there's enough down here to show what's been
              going on. The handwriting's disguised, of course
              – but I've had it checked by experts. This and the
              suicide note were written by one and the same man
              . . . Howard Holt.

KAREN   Even if all this were true, it still doesn't prove the
              girl's alive.

DAVIES   No. But in the circumstances, can you afford to
              admit she's dead?

              (*She is cornered. The telephone rings. She
              answers it.*)

KAREN   Hello? (*Holds it out.*) It's for you.

DAVIES   Thank you. (*Takes it.*) Yes? (*Listens.*) Right – I'll
              come straight down.

              (*He hangs up.*)

DAVIES   We've got her, Mrs Holt. Sergeant Briggs has just
              picked her up.

KAREN   You knew all along she was alive?

DAVIES   We suspected it. You see, her father got a
              money-order from her in the middle of September,
              two weeks after she disappeared, and she was the
              only one involved who knew of his existence. I
              tackled Mr Holt on that point and it gave him quite
              a shock. We felt that if Julie and your husband
              were working together on this she'd try and

contact you as soon as she heard of his death.
With that in mind, we made the suicide front-page
news . . . in all the *London* papers.

(*He nods towards* JULIE'S *paper.*)

KAREN   You were watching for her?

DAVIES   Aye. She turned up sooner than we expected.
             Luckily, Will Purdie spotted her and gave us a
             ring. I told him to get up here and keep his eyes
             skinned.

KAREN   So that's why he came.

DAVIES   And why I followed. She was too quick for the pair
             of us. It was old Tom Briggs who got her, in the
             end.

KAREN   Just – one old country policeman.

DAVIES   (*quietly*) I'll have to ask you to come with me, Mrs
             Holt.

(*She still has a card to play.*)

KAREN   May I ask on what charge you're arresting me?

DAVIES   I'm not arresting you. But I want your statement,
             along with Julie Grant's.

KAREN   The girl's alive. My husband used her for his own
             purposes. What does that prove?

DAVIES   Only what a fool he was to kill himself when he
             knew all along there'd be no murder charge.

KAREN   She rang through yesterday and threatened to
             expose him, because of that he took his own life.

DAVIES   Then why did he write, "I killed Julie Grant"?

KAREN   There must be other reasons –

DAVIES   Name them!

KAREN   I can't! You can't expect me to look into a dead man's mind!

DAVIES   Isn't it more likely that when I telephoned he thought we'd picked the girl up in London and she'd talked? He tried to break with you, to get away – and you shot him!

KAREN   Prove it!

DAVIES   I wish I could.

KAREN   You haven't an atom of proof that he intended to leave this house.

(The telephone rings.)

KAREN   Carry on, Inspector – you've taken charge here!

(She deliberately turns her back on him as he picks it up.)

DAVIES   Hello? Yes. Oh, yes? What time was that? Thank you. Yes, put it through by all means.

(He hangs up and feels for his pipe.)

DAVIES   At six o'clock last night, your husband died by shooting. Ten minutes before that, he booked a seat on the night plane to Amsterdam.

(She stands, turned to stone.)

KAREN   The one thing I overlooked. He said he'd made arrangements. The only time he ever spoke the truth and I didn't believe him.

DAVIES   That was from the airport. They were wondering in the circumstances if you'd mind settling the account.

KAREN   It won't be the first I've paid for him.

DAVIES   It may be the last.

KAREN   Not – quite.

             (*She has lost.*)

KAREN   All right, Inspector. I offered him money in return
             for a confession and shot him as he signed it.

DAVIES   Revenge, was it – for the girl?

KAREN   Not that alone. I made a man die because he
             wasn't fit to live. You call that murder – I prefer to
             think of it as justifiable homicide.

DAVIES   (*gets her coat*) You'll be formally charged at the
             station. The car's outside.

             (*He helps her into her coat.*)

KAREN   Thank you.

             (*She crosses to the door.*)

DAVIES   (*feels for matches*) No tricks –

KAREN   I wouldn't try to get away.

DAVIES   You wouldn't stand much chance, would you?

KAREN   (*at door*) When you come to think of it . . . I never
             did.

             (*She goes off. DAVIES lingers only long enough to
             strike a match, and then he follows. As he leaves,
             he is lighting his pipe . . . at last.*)

             (*Blackout.*)

PROPERTY PLOT

ACT ONE

Set on Desk:	Matches.
	Writing paper holder, back C.
	Headed paper and envelopes, in holder.
	Ink stand (with ink), below holder.
	Photo of HOWARD in frame, US.
	Photo of KAREN in matching frame, DS.
	Blotter (with folding side-leaves), C.
	Coloured blotting paper, in blotter.
	Cheap blue writing paper, in C drawer.
	Fountain pen, on ink stand.
	Telephone (not dial), US.
	Telephone Directory (Chelmsford Area),
	    DS of telephone.
	Silver cigarette box, DS of KAREN's photo.
	Scissors, Top US drawer.
	Table lighter, US of ink stand.
	Scissors, Top US drawer.
	Table lighter, US of ink stand.
	Ashtray (large), between telephone and
	    blotter.
	Paper-knife, between ink stand and blotter.

Set on Table RC:	JULIE's bag, with lighter and cigarette
	    case containing one cork-tipped
	    cigarette, ashtray.

Set on Sofa Table:	Two magazines (one open). Ashtray on open magazine.
Set on floor below DL Chair:	Two sheets of typing paper. Red book (open, face down).
Set in Safe:	Seven blackmail letter (stamped and postmarked, cheap blue stationery). Long bank envelope, containing money. Revolver (00.32).

Set on Drinks Table:	Whisky (practical), L of large glasses. Brandy (practical), L end of tray. Gin, UL corner of tray. Sherry decanter, UR corner of tray. Soda syphon (practical), above whisky. Seven large glasses, R end of tray. Three small glasses, round brandy. Bottle opener, DS edge of tray. Ashtray, DC on tray.
Set on UR Table:	Flower vase.
Set on Window Sill:	Pile of typing paper.
Set Near Desk:	Wastepaper basket, DS of desk.
Set on DL Chair:	Typewriter, with sheet of typing paper in it. HOWARD'S raincoat, with car keys in R pocket, lying over back of chair.
Set off R:	One small bottle of stout. Bunch of chrysanthemums, in tissue paper. KAREN'S shopping bag. MISS CUNNINGHAM'S shopping basket with library books. Small bunch of flowers. Letters to post. Cigarettes. HOWARD'S brown leather briefcase. Two scripts. Passport. Unsealed blackmail letter (stamped but not postmarked). DAVIES'S black official briefcase. Documents. Pipe. KAREN'S black handbag.
Set off L:	Two bottles of beer (dark glass, half-pint). Pewter tankard. Empty glass on small tray.

Morning paper (folded to conceal title).
KAREN's weekend case and coat.

Note:

US window open.
Curtains shut.
Doors shut.
Radio on.

ACT TWO

Scene One

Strike:

One glass from sofa table.
One glass from desk.
One glass from drinks table.
Beer bottle from RC table.
Tankard from drinks table.
Torn up cigarette from sofa table.
KAREN's handbag from sofa table.
Book and typing paper from floor.

Reset:

Telephone directory.
Desk chair right in to desk.
Magazines tidied on sofa table.

Set on Desk:

Letters to post.
Cigarettes in box.
Typewriter.

Set on RC Table:

Duster.

Check:

Scissors.
Table lighter.
Vase.
Wastepaper basket.
Chrysanthemums.
KAREN's shopping bag.
MISS CUNNINGHAM's shopping basket.
Magazines on sofa table, C of it.

Note:

Curtains open.
US window open.
Doors shut.

ACT TWO

Scene Two

Strike:	Flower from drinks table.
Set:	Desk ashtray to US end of desk.
	Open blotter.
	Cheap writing paper from C drawer to blotter.
	Pen on blotter.
	Typewriter on US end of sofa.
	Typing paper from windowsill to C of sofa.
	Cigarettes.
	Desk ashtray.
	Pen.
	Lighter.
	Whisky.
	Two glasses.
	Wastepaper basket.
	Empty glass on tray.
	Small bunch of flowers.
Note:	Curtains open.
	US window open.
	Doors shut.

ACT THREE

Scene One

Strike:	Flowers from wastepaper basket.
	Two dirty glasses from drinks table.
Reset:	Desk chair right in to desk.
	US leaf of blotter open.
	Paper-knife on closed leaf of blotter, handle facing in-stage.

Set on Desk:	Two scripts, DS of blotter.
	HOWARD's briefcase, US edge of blotter.
	Passport, C of blotter.
	Unsealed blackmail letter, below
	ink stand.
Set over RC Chair:	HOWARD's coat.
Set on Drinks Tray:	Glass of brandy for KAREN.
Check:	Paper-knife.
	Pen.
	Headed writing paper.
	Letters in safe.
	Revolver in safe.
Collect:	DAVIES's hat, for scene drop.
Note:	Curtains shut.
	US window open.
	Doors shut.

ACT THREE

Scene Two

Strike:	Blackmail envelope from desk.
	Crumpled blackmail letter from floor.
	Revolver from desk.
	Confession from desk.
	One glass from sofa table.
	HOWARD's briefcase.
	HOWARD's coat.
	Desk chair slightly out from desk.
	Paper-knife on desk.
Set on Desk:	DAVIES's briefcase.
	Documents.
	Pipe.
	KAREN's black handbag.
Set on UR Table:	DAVIES's hat.
Check:	KAREN's weekend case and coat.

Morning paper.
Envelope of money in safe.

Note: Curtains open.
US window open.
Doors shut.
Safe closed, and picture in position.

PERSONAL PROPS

KAREN

Give: 50p, for MISS CUNNINGHAM.
Driving licence.
Two cigarettes.
Handbag, brown leather.

Check (in bag):   Powder compact.
Handkerchief.
Comb.
Latch key.
Folder, brown leather, with insurance
    certificate and compartment for licence.

Collect: Coat for Act Three, Scene 2.
Second handbag (black).

DAVIES

Check: Wallet with money, cards, etc.
Photograph of JULIE (postcard size).
Folded piece of blotting paper (to match
    that in blotter), with ink impression of
    part of blackmail letter.
Notebook.
Pencil, with clip.
Pipe.
Smoker's penknife, with pipe-cleaning
    attachments,
Tobacco and matches.

Collect: Second pipe.

Howard

Give: Two cigarettes.
        First blackmail letter.

Check: Handkerchief.
        Cigarette case and lighter.

Collect: Coat.

Miss Cunningham

Check: Shoulder bag.

       In bag: Receipt book.
            Ball point pen.
            Purse.

Collect: 50p.

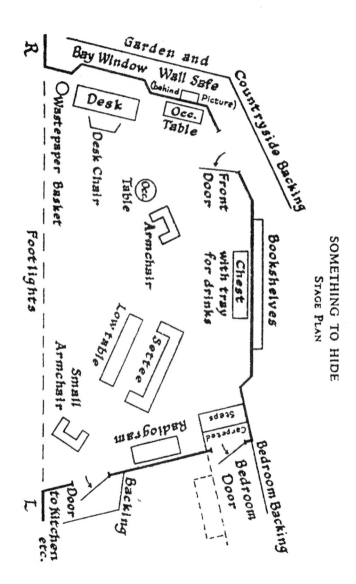

SOMETHING TO HIDE
STAGE PLAN